MW00777599

"On one level, Scriptura practice of scriptural st traditions. On another level, SR names a unique type of reasoning that emerges from such study, especially within small groups that have practiced SR study over many months. Only a few SR thinkers have explored the relation of this reasoning to the academic disciplines. Jacob Goodson has taken the next, significant step: hosting a veritable symposium of SR thinkers in dialogue with well-known Western philosophers from Hegel to Eco. The result is a book of equally high imagination and sharp philosophic analysis, single-handedly projecting the reasoning of SR into mainstream philosophic discourse. A stunning achievement."

—**Peter Ochs**, University of Virginia

"An exceptionally fine introduction to Scriptural Reasoning without sacrificing intellectual rigor and attention to detail. The discussions of Peirce, Ricoeur, and Habermas, as well as those of Kant, Hegel, and Coleridge, place the practice of scriptural reasoning in a long Western tradition of reasoning out of texts. Goodson's lucid expositions will be welcomed by readers who have not undertaken firsthand study of the philosophical texts. He beautifully captures the apparent contradictions of scriptural reasoning: it both has goals and refuses to be goal driven; it both invites theoretical reflection and resists any single theoretical account from a single tradition. Anyone who is curious about the intellectual currents that run through scriptural reasoning is well served by this excellent study."

—**Nicholas Adams**, University of Birmingham

"At a time of great strife and fundamentalism, it is imperative to understand different religious traditions with academic clarity. Scriptural reasoning is a beautiful practice that allows Jewish, Muslim, and Christian thinkers to address the topics that lie at the core of humanity with a clarity of thought and an openness of heart. The first comprehensive book on SR's history, technique, and application, Goodson guides us into a new way to have old conversations."

—**Brad Elliott Stone**, Loyola Marymount University

The Philosopher's Playground

The Philosopher's Playground

Understanding Scriptural Reasoning
through Modern Philosophy

Jacob L. Goodson

CASCADE *Books* • Eugene, Oregon

THE PHILOSOPHER'S PLAYGROUND
Understanding Scriptural Reasoning through Modern Philosophy

Cascade Books
An Imprint of Wipf and Stock Publishers
199 W. 8th Ave., Suite 3
Eugene, OR 97401

www.wipfandstock.com

PAPERBACK ISBN: 978-1-60899-558-5
HARDCOVER ISBN: 978-1-4982-8608-4
EBOOK ISBN: 978-1-7252-4564-8

Cataloguing-in-Publication data:

Names: Goodson, Jacob L., author.

Title: The philosopher's playground : understanding scriptural reasoning through modern philosophy / by Jacob L. Goodson.

Description: Eugene, OR : Cascade Books, 2021 | Includes bibliographical references and index(es).

Identifiers: ISBN 978-1-60899-558-5 (paperback) | ISBN 978-1-4982-8608-4 (hardcover) | ISBN 978-1-7252-4564-8 (ebook)

Subjects: LCSH: Bible—Criticism, interpretation, etc., Jewish, Christian, and Islamic.

Classification: BL71 .G66 2021 (print) | BL71 .G66 (ebook)

The Introduction quotes extensively from Mike Higton and Rachel Muers, *Text in Play: Experiments in Reading Scripture*, (Cascade Books, 2012). Used by permission.

11/05/21

Dedicated to those in the Scriptural Reasoning
Academic Network, especially:

Kevin Seidel, Sara Williams,
and Matthew Vaughan

GLAUCON: How would you arrange goods—are there not some which we welcome for their own sakes, independently of their consequences? For example, harmless pleasures and enjoyments—which delight us at certain times, even if nothing follows from them?

SOCRATES: I agree in thinking there is such a class.

GLAUCON: Is there not also a second class of goods—such as knowledge, health, our senses? They are desirable in themselves and because they have definite good results.

SOCRATES: Certainly.

GLAUCON: And would you not recognize a third class—such as caring for the sick, which is the physician's art, and various ways of making money? These are good but only because of the consequence or result that they lead to. No one would choose it for its own sake, but only for the sake of some result or reward that follows from them.

SOCRATES: There is this third class too.

—Plato, *Republic*, Book II

Contents

Contents

Acknowledgments

Charlie Collier contracted this book over ten years ago, and I simply could not write most of it until my first professional Sabbatical in 2020. Each November, I would give him reasons why it was not yet completed; he never suggested that we walk away from the project. I am grateful for his patience and trust.

Peter Ochs read through the manuscript immediately after I completed it. We met on a weekly basis via Zoom to discuss each chapter individually. The guidance and wisdom in his weekly responses has greatly increased the quality of the book. Mistakes remain my responsibility.

I appreciate the feedback on certain chapters from colleagues, friends, and students. The following people offered editorial comments, full responses, or general suggestions to (at least) one of the chapters in this book: Morgan Elbot (University of Memphis), Nauman Faizi (Lahore University), Randy Friedman (Binghamton University), Mark James (Hunter College), Jackson Lashier (Southwestern College), David O'Hara (Augustana University), John Shook

(University of Buffalo), Brad Stone (Loyola Marymount University), Matthew Vaughan (Columbia University), and Willie Young (Endicott College). I specify in the chapters themselves who helped with which chapter.

Abbreviations

CW   David F. Ford, *Christian Wisdom: Desiring God and Learning in Love*

HMI   Daniel Hardy, "Harmony and Mutual Implication in the *Opus Maximum*"

HT   Nicholas Adams, *Habermas and Theology*

MDRP   Nicholas Adams, "Making Deep Reasonings Public"

PPLS   Peter Ochs, *Peirce, Pragmatism, and the Logic of Scripture*

PSI   Peter Ochs, "An Introduction to Postcritical Scriptural Interpretation"

PSR   Daniel Hardy, "The Promise of Scriptural Reasoning"

PWSR   Peter Ochs, "Philosophic Warrants for Scriptural Reasoning"

Abbreviations

RRTI	Muhammad Iqbal, *The Reconstruction of Religious Thought in Islam*
RSR	Marianne Moyaert, "Ricoeur, Interreligious Literacy, and Scriptural Reasoning"
RWIS	Daniel Hardy, "Reason, Wisdom and the Interpretation of Scripture"
RWV	Peter Ochs, *Religion without Violence: On the Philosophy and Practice of Scriptural Reasoning*
TP	Mike Higton and Rachel Muers, *The Text in Play: Experiments in Reading Scripture*

Introduction

This book invites readers to think about the practice of Scriptural Reasoning (SR) in relation to late modern philosophy, American pragmatism, and postmodernism. Because SR remains difficult to write about (for reasons that will be articulated throughout the book), I focus on the philosophical moves and sources that illuminate the *how* and *why* of SR. In other words, I take the order of the phrase as a guide to writing about the practice: *reasoning* as the substantive with *scriptural* as its modifier. The result of this decision is that while this book talks about the practice of SR, it also offers a tour through modern philosophy—not chronologically but thematically. In this sense, this book could be used in an undergraduate philosophy classroom that covers themes or topics such as cultivating friendship, inter-faith dialogue, hermeneutics and theories of interpretation, the role of Scripture within philosophy, versions of rationality and reason, and what wisdom might mean in the twenty-first century.

I have divided the sections based upon questions that I receive about SR. In Part 1, I address the question: What is *scriptural* about Scriptural Reasoning? In Part 2, I address the question: What is the *reasoning* of Scriptural Reasoning? In Part 3, I address questions concerning the relational dynamics involved with SR.

As stated in the first paragraph, this book also offers a tour through modern philosophy.[1] Individual chapters could have been named based upon such a tour (what follows differs from the table of contents):

Chapter 1. C. S. Peirce's Pragmatism and Semiotics

Chapter 2. Paul Ricoeur on Wisdom

Chapter 3. Samuel Taylor Coleridge's Romanticism

Chapter 4. Mahummed Iqbal on Religious Reasoning

Chapter 5. Jürgen Habermas on Communicative Rationality

Chapter 6. Martha Nussbaum on Friendship, Luck, Vulnerability

Chapter 7. G. W. F. Hegel on the Problem of Interfaith Dialogues

Chapter 8. John Caputo on Hope, Postmodern Playfulness, and Radical Hermeneutics

In the conclusion, I give a decisively Kantian description of the practice of SR. I intend for this tour to be helpful in explaining the *how* and *why* of SR, as well as being useful pedagogically. Later in this Introduction, I say more about how this philosophical tour aids us in better understanding the practice of SR.

---

1. I direct readers to Chris Hackett's excellent essay on the Cartesian aspects of SR as well, which are not addressed by me in this project; see Hackett, "Clasp of the Catena."

It turned out to be quite difficult to write this book. Because of certain limitations, choices had to be made in relation to which philosophers to implement for explaining SR. For instance, I am more comfortable and knowledgeable in writing about the French philosopher Emmanuel Levinas than I am writing about the French philosopher Paul Ricoeur. However, Robert Gibbs has a clearly written essay on Levinas and SR, whereas Ricoeur's philosophy remains significant yet somewhat vague within David Ford's explanation of SR.[2]

Another instance that proved a difficult choice: one plan for this book was simply to commit chapters to each of the "rules" of SR—developed most clearly and thoroughly by Steven Kepnes of Colgate University.[3] I decided, however, such an approach would make neither for an interesting philosophical read, nor could I improve upon Kepnes's and others' "rules" for SR.[4] Some of these rules, of course, get stated throughout the book, but only as they arise organically within the contours of the philosophical argument being presented. In the conclusion, I reduce the practice of SR down to two rules based upon Kant's tests of dignity and universalization.

SR and a Sense of Strangeness

SR started as a practice in 1994 as a result of adding Christian theologians to the already existing practice called Textual Reasoning (TR)—a group of Jewish scholars who studied their own sacred texts and commentaries on those texts together. Eventually, they decided to include a

---

2. See Gibbs, "Reading with Others," 171–84.

3. See Kepnes, "Handbook for Scriptural Reasoning," 23–39.

4. For the others' rules, see Elkins and Richardson, *Journal of Scriptural Reasoning.*

graduate student and practicing Muslim in their times of study—making the participation Jewish, Christian, *and* Muslim. The names often associated as the original crew of SR are David Ford, Daniel Hardy, Basit Koshul, and Peter Ochs. Others from Textual Reasoning included Robert Gibbs, Steven Kepnes, and Laurie Zoloth. United Methodist pastor and theologian William Wesley Elkins also was part of the beginnings of SR as a practice. Initially, the practice flourished in the state of New Jersey: both at Drew University and Princeton University. This initial group started doing SR at the international meeting known as the American Academy of Religion (AAR), which greatly enlarged the circle of SR practitioners. Eventually, both Cambridge University and the University of Virginia (UVa) formulated ways to practice and study SR: Ford and Hardy at Cambridge and Ochs at UVa.

Fuller histories of SR have been written elsewhere, and for this book I choose to do what Peter Ochs always encouraged me to do in his office as a graduate student: articulate my own history and reasons for writing about what I write about.[5] I came to UVa in August 2005 to study American Philosophy with Professor Peter Ochs. In April 2006, he agreed to mentor me through the PhD program. As part of this, he wanted me to practice SR and work with SR groups in both the UK and the US. However, this was not my initiation into SR.

At an American Academy of Religion meeting in Atlanta, Georgia—before knowing who Ochs was or reading any of his work on the American Philosopher, Charles

5. Among his doctoral students, Ochs was known for a psychoanalytic approach for choosing research topics and subject matters for a dissertation: articulating the autobiographical reasons for why one wishes to spend their time researching a particular question was as important, in the context of meeting with Ochs, as the content of the particular question.

Sanders Peirce—I stumbled into a session that looked vastly different than any of the other sessions I had attended. The year was 2003, and I was in Atlanta to give a paper on William James's *Varieties of Religious Experience*. Because of my strong sense of curiosity, in addition to presenting, I packed my days attending sessions and listening to papers.

For those who have never attended an AAR meeting, most of the sessions are in smaller rooms with chairs lined up in rows; also, a podium and table are usually up front for the presenters. Most sessions involve the presenters reading papers that they have written on a topic relating to the theme of the session. These details may seem unnecessary to give, but they become necessary for understanding SR as a particular and peculiar kind of *practice*—indeed, a *strange practice*—at least in relation to other academic and scholarly practices.

I walked into a session at nine o'clock on a Sunday night in November 2003. My memory fails me concerning my motives, but I imagine I ended up there mainly because it was one of only a few options given the late time. The room was quite large. Instead of chairs in rows, the room was set up with round tables—and about nine to ten chairs per table. Like the other meeting rooms, there was a podium with a table toward the front of the room. Like other sessions at the AAR, this session had three presenters; unlike other AAR sessions, these presenters did not read papers but talked "on their feet" (as academics say) about scriptural passages relating to Adam—as in the biblical characters Adam and Eve.

Once the presenters completed their thoughts (I was unaware at the time that they were offering a *plain sense* interpretation of passages about Adam from Genesis, Paul's epistles, and the Qur'an), we were told to discuss *the texts in front of us* with those at our table. I had not encountered this requirement at any other academic conference, and

I—a twenty-three-year-old from Oklahoma, now living in Chicago, and trying to fit in at a 12,000-person conference in Atlanta—found myself at a table with Christians, Jews, *and* Muslims. Furthermore, these scholars *identified* as Christian, Jewish, and Muslim—which surprised me because I had been warned by teachers not to identify my own religious background at the AAR. Our group had a moderator (I do not know who, but it could have been someone who I now consider a close friend) who surprised me by challenging, disagreeing, and questioning every claim made—no matter who made it or what was stated by that person. I remained silent but eventually the moderator looked directly at me and said, "You've been quiet: What do you see happening in these texts?"

I have blocked the memory of what I said in response, but I do remember being completely fascinated by the conversation everyone else was having at the table—sometimes not knowing what was going on, but other times recognizing how some of the claims directly contradicted or related to what I learned about the biblical character Adam growing up as a Southern Baptist Christian. There was much excitement and spirit in the room, and I allowed myself to eavesdrop on the groups closest to us in order to hear the directions of their conversations as well (sometimes, within SR, it becomes difficult to be fully present in your own study group because of other fascinating conversations taking place in the same room).

We were told over and over again to focus our attention on the three passages in front of us. Those three passages involved very small selections from the first part of Genesis, Paul's Epistles, and the Qur'an. It would have been my first time reading any passage from the Qur'an, and I remember being so mesmerized by the words of the Muslim participants at the table. I might have said only the one sentence—which, again, I have blocked from memory—but I learned a great deal about the character of Adam during the ninety-minute discussion.

One distinct memory I have concerns a debate that arose between the moderator and what seemed to be one of the Christian participants: the participant started to generalize about human nature based upon what the Genesis and Pauline passages stated about Adam. The moderator quickly challenged him (two men were partaking in this debate): "In SR, we do not generalize but stay with the particularity of the characters of the text." To which the participant rebutted, "But the theme of the session is 'human anthropology', which means that the session wants us to generalize about human nature." The moderator responded, "Well, at this table, we are not going to generalize about human nature because as readers we tend to be too conceptualist; SR allows us to repair that tendency by staying with the particularity of the character and logic of the three Scriptures." Admittedly, this went way over my head at the time; however, I carried it around with me and continued to think about that specific debate. The ways in which SR addresses this tension between particularity and generality will be addressed in this book.

The session came to a close around 11:00 with another presenter (not listed on the program) standing up to talk about why he thinks SR is such an important practice. I did not know who he was at the time, but I met him a few years later when he visited UVa during my time as a graduate student there. It was Daniel Hardy (now of blessed memory), and when meeting him at UVa I immediately placed him as the speaker who concluded the SR session on Adam in Atlanta. In some ways, on that late night in Atlanta, he used jargon that I had heard growing up in an American Evangelical Christian culture (Southern Baptists in Oklahoma consider themselves American Evangelicals): "Scripture is sacred," "the spirit is with us tonight," "and when two or more are gathered, there I am [Jesus] also." In other ways, however, he sounded *so different* than American Evangelical Christianity: claiming Christians needed to be with Muslims to know and to learn about God; plus saying that Christians, Jews, and Muslims reading and studying their sacred texts together is the future for religious traditions to survive and thrive.

I tell this story from my early twenties to give a sense of what the practice of SR feels and looks like. In sum, the practice of SR involves (a) people of different religious traditions arguing over and trying to make sense of small passages from texts that some consider Scripture and some do not;[6] (b) debates arise, during the activity, about methodology and ways of reading; and (c) participants are asked to speak if/when they remain quiet or silent during a SR session. As we will learn throughout the course of this book, there is much more to SR than these three features. My inclination, however, is that the sense of strangeness I felt in 2003 offers readers a personal sense of what the practice of SR feels and looks like.[7]

6. Or, in Gary Slater's more eloquent words, "Peter Ochs's Scriptural Reasoning [project] understands the logic of scriptural interpretation as a process of applying religious insights to their appropriate contexts, a process that is enhanced when members of different faith traditions interpret each other's sacred texts together." Slater, *C. S. Peirce and the Nested Continua Model*, 114.

7. Basit Koshul also describes SR in terms of its strangeness: "I had come to know a group of 'strangers' and many new 'strange' ideas. David Ford was among this group of 'strangers,' along with Peter Ochs and Daniel Hardy (of blessed memory). . . . And while I was familiar with interfaith dialogue at that time, the idea of Scriptural Reasoning was also 'strange.' Furthermore, while I was familiar with Christianity and Judaism to some degree, these traditions were also 'strange' in a very real sense because my relationship with a living

SR and Taking a Tour through
Modern Philosophy

In this section, I preview the chapters in more detail than I did at beginning of this introduction. In chapter 1, I will read the American pragmatist philosopher C. S. Peirce through Peter Ochs—one of the founders of SR—in order to establish why a philosopher "returns to Scripture" as part of their philosophical work.[8] I compare and contrast Ochs's interpretation of Peirce with interpretations from other Peirce scholars; namely, Robert Corrington, Umberto Eco, and William Rogers. Also in chapter 1, I introduce the main tension concerning the practice of SR that interests me most: semiotics vs. pragmatism. In later chapters, I refer to this tension under different names: playfulness vs. purposefulness (ch. 2), and musement vs. theological seriousness (ch. 3). Another way to state this tension is in the form of a question: Is SR strictly a playful practice that has no definite ends or outcomes, or should SR be considered a practice with a definite purpose (such as friendship, interreligious peace, and/or the survival of religious traditions)? In Ochs's account of SR, this tension involves Peirce's pragmatism versus his semiotics.

Chapters 1 and 2 are tied together because they both articulate the role of Scripture within the practice of Scriptural Reasoning. In chapter 2, I clarify the role of Paul Ricoeur's philosophy in David Ford's theology—more particularly, Ford's use of Ricoeur to offer a theological defense and description of the practice of SR. Like Peirce, Ricouer

---

Christian or Jew did not go beyond institutional formality or collegiality." Koshul, "Theology as a Vocation," 211–12.

8. The phrase "return to Scripture" is between quotation marks because Ochs edited a whole volume around what the phrase means in Christian theology and Jewish philosophy; see Ochs, *Return to Scripture in Judaism and Christianity*.

also "returns to Scripture" as part of his philosophical work; somewhat differently from Peirce, however, Ricouer's "return to Scripture" seems motivated mostly by the types of wisdom found within the Christian canon.[9] I rely on Marianne Moyaert's essay on Ricouer and SR to make clear and explicit the role of Ricoeur's philosophy within the practice of SR. I conclude chapter 2 by returning to the main tension within SR, and I demonstrate that Ford's account of SR falls on the side of playfulness over purposefulness.

In the second part of this book, I explore types of reasonings involved with the practice of Scriptural Reasoning. In chapter 3, I read the British Romantic philosopher Samuel Taylor Coleridge through Daniel Hardy—another one of the founders of SR—in order to understand the theological rationale for SR. One of Hardy's main points about SR concerns how it must be a practice with purposefulness and theological seriousness.

Chapters 1 through 3 cover the three founders of SR, as well as the philosophical theories that contribute to how the founders reflect upon the practice of SR. In chapter 4, however, I focus more exclusively on the work of a modern philosopher—in this case, the Pakistani philosopher Muhammad Iqbal. I argue that Iqbal provides three terms for understanding the *reasoning process* within the practice of SR: faith, thought, discovery. When Iqbal talks about how this process depicts religious reasoning and applies it to religious life, he means it with *theological seriousness*; when I transfer Iqbal's reconstruction of religious reasoning to the practice of Scriptural Reasoning, however, I think that it becomes a *playful reasoning process*—a process that

9. I do not mean to suggest that Peirce does not find wisdom in Scripture; rather, Ricoeur deeply emphasizes "biblical wisdom" as a category whereas I do not locate that phrase in Peirce's work.

involves argumentation, critical engagement, and self-criticism—with no definite ends required.

In chapter 4, I read the German philosopher Jürgen Habermas through Nicholas Adams—who has become one of the more prolific writers on questions concerning the practice of SR. Adams uses the phrase, "making deep reasonings public," as a primary descriptor for the practice of SR.[10] Because of the relational dynamics of SR—which is the heading of the third part of this book—I argue that *discovering* becomes a better verb than *making* for the ways in which Adams uses Habermas's theory of communicative rationality for understanding SR. In chapter 4, I claim that SR becomes a playful practice that helps participants *discover* their "deep reasonings" no matter how broken religious traditions seem to be in the modern world.[11] For Adams, however, SR is not a playful practice but a purposeful practice with a definite end—the end or goal of friendship.

Continuing with the theme of the relational dynamics in the practice of SR, I look to the work of Martha Nussbaum to offer SR theorists a model of what friendship looks like if friendship remains one of the goals or purposes of SR. Although I am skeptical of making friendship one of the aims of the practice of SR, as the author of a book explaining the practice, I feel obligated to think through what kind of friendships SR makes possible. Because of her emphasis on fragility, luck, and vulnerability, I argue that Nussbaum's account of *philia* (love) proves the most realistic and reasonable version of friendship for SR. Chapters 6 and 7 represent my best attempt to defend SR as a practice with a purpose—the purpose being the cultivation of inter-religious friendships based on *philia* (ch. 6) and Hegelian *xenophilia* (ch. 7).

10. See Adams, MDRP, 41–57.

11. See Adams, MDRP, 41–57.

Introduction

What is the best name for the practice of SR? Throughout the book, I call SR an inter-religious dialogue—a name
which goes unchallenged, and I will continue to call SR an
inter-religious dialogue in everyday conversations about
SR.[12] After re-reading one of the giants of modern philosophy—G. W. F. Hegel—on what faith means in modernity,
I have decided to strongly question labeling SR an "inter-
faith dialogue." One of the themes that runs throughout
this book concerns how *the practice of SR repairs the problem of xenophobia* in the modern world, and I use Hegel's
philosophy of religion to show how such a repair ought to
lead to *xenophilia*—which builds from and relates to the application of Nussbaum's account of *philia* to the practice of
SR established in chapter 6.

Chapter 8 continues exploring the question of the
best name for the practice of SR. In his memoir about his
philosophical development, John Caputo introduces the
phrase inter-hope dialogue as a potential replacement for
inter-faith dialogue. I consider the ways in which the practices of SR differs from and looks like Caputo's version of an
inter-hope dialogue.

In the conclusion, I return to the modern philosopher
par excellence Immanuel Kant and use his deontological
reasoning to reduce or simplify the "rules" of SR down to
two: one rule that follows the logic of the dignity test, and
one rule that follows the logic of the universalization test.
For the sake of simplicity, I keep the conclusion brief.

12. For the clearest and most thorough account of SR as an inter-
religious dialogue, see Moyaert, "Scriptural Reasoning as Inter-Religious Dialogue," 64–86. I cannot improve upon Moyaert's argument.

Socrates and the Problem
of Writing about SR

A final question needs to be addressed in this introduction, and this question is best expressed as a philosophical problem: Perhaps SR should not be written about at all? I noted toward the beginning of this introduction that this book on SR has proven difficult to write. Perhaps this difficulty signals a deeper problem?

One of the founders of SR, David Ford, writes a lot about SR and simultaneously warns against writing about SR! Ford states the problem by returning to an argument made by Socrates and represented by Plato in his dialogue, *Phaedrus*.[13] Ford claims that when trying to write about SR, "[o]ne is reminded of Plato on the dangers and disadvantages of writing over against live conversations."[14] Since SR sessions are "live conversations," Ford reasons, "it is extremely hard to do justice in print to the complex oral exchanges of small groups studying three scriptures at once, and even harder for one person to do so."[15]

While I am "one person" trying "to do justice in print to the complex oral exchanges of small groups studying three scriptures at once,"[16] I do so only in relation to the reflections and work of others in regard to SR. In fact, this book could not have been written without being intellectually formed by three major studies on SR (and its related practice, Textual Reasoning)—only one of which I actually cite and engage with in this book. The study I cite and

13. See Plato, *Phaedrus*. For the parts of the dialogue where Socrates dismisses the activity of writing, see 275C, 275D, 275E, 276C, 277D.

14. Ford, *CW*, 297–98.

15. Ford, *CW*, 296.

16. Ford, *CW*, 296.

engage with in the book, which I recommend readers of this book also read, is Mike Higton's and Rachel Muers's "What Is Scriptural Reasoning? How Christians, Jews, and Muslims Can Read Together" in their book, *The Text in Play: Experiments in Reading Scripture.*[17]

Higton and Muers provide a fictional dialogue that resembles what some SR sessions actually sound like. I offer a sample of their fictional dialogue here. The set-up: after discussing the burning bush passage found in Exodus, chapter 3, the group turns toward a discussion of Surah 40:78 in the Qur'an:

> We sent Messengers before thee; of some We have related to thee, and some We have not related to thee. It was not for any Messenger to bring a sign, save by God's leave. When God's command comes, justly the issue shall be decided; then the vain-doers shall be lost.[18]

Based upon Exodus 3 and Surah 40:78, Higton and Muers imagine a SR session sounding like this between six participants:

> NATHAN: I wanted to come back to the point about the vain-doers' responsibility. Is there a sense in which the vain-doers have closed themselves off, so it's not simply a matter of a decision, in the moment when they are confronted by the sign, to reject that sign, but of that being a decision for which they have perversely prepared themselves? They've prepared themselves to ignore transparency . . .

17. See my "appreciative review" of their book: Goodson, "What Should I Read to Learn about Scriptural Reasoning?"

18. Arberry, *Koran Interpreted*, 40:78.

BRIAN: They've immunized themselves against the contagion?

HABIB: The vain-doers are not simply all those who did not understand this particular sign . . .

KAREN: My translation has "the followers of falsehood," which sounds more like a pattern of life than a one-off decision.

AALIYAH: Yes, they are people who have told themselves that the world they see is all there is . . .

NATHAN: That there is only surface, and no depth?

AALIYAH: Yes . . .

HABIB: But you shouldn't lose the sense of responsibility that remains at the time when the sign is actually given. Signs—in God's wisdom—they do . . . break through to people and confront them. God gives people signs that are fit for their context, fit to communicate to them. When a sign comes, it is powerful and active . . .

KAREN: It passes true judgment.

HABIB: Yes, but it also is not so overwhelming as to deprive you of responsibility. A sign comes close to you, but also leaves some distance; you will hear it, but you are responsible for acceptance or rejection. You're not deprived of your humanity in the process.

AALIYAH: And even Muhammad has to seek confirmation: the message he receives does not stop him from asking questions and doubting himself, or from knowing that he is human.

MORGAN: So a sign that comes to someone who has closed themselves off against the potential transparency of things—against the more-than-visible—is going to have to be something visible that nevertheless shakes them out of that . . .

NATHAN: Like the burning bush in the text we were looking at last time[?]

MORGAN: Yes.

BRIAN: Which also leaves Moses needing confirmation—leaves him human and questioning and unsure.[19]

Notice how much discussion they achieve over the phrase vain-doers: What does it mean to be a vain-doer? Who can become one? How does someone become a vain-doer? Is it a one-time choice or a way of life? After working through all of these questions, they connect Surah 40:78 with the burning bush narrative in Exodus 3—which they had discussed previously to Surah 40:78. In addition to my earlier report concerning my initial experience of SR in 2003 of what SR feels and looks like, Higton and Muers's fictional dialogue gives a sense of what the practice sounds like. I recommend readers of this book check out the full dialogue they provide in their study of SR.[20]

Another major study on SR that has formed and shaped me intellectually is Matthew Vaughan's dissertation, "Scriptural Reasoning as Interreligious Education."[21]

19. Higton and Muers, *TP*, 105–6.

20. Especially if you are reading this book and have never practiced SR, see Higton and Muers, *TP*, 96–109.

21. See Vaughan, "Scriptural Reasoning as (Inter)Religious Education." I served as the external member of Vaughan's dissertation committee.

Vaughan provides a similar picture of SR that I provide in this book, with the difference being that his dissertation focuses on SR as a certain type of pedagogy whereas I emphasize the philosophical aspects of SR. For those readers who want to implement SR as a pedagogical practice, Vaughan's dissertation is a must-read!

Lastly, the essays that comprise Nancy Levene's and Peter Ochs's *Textual Reasonings: Jewish Philosophy and Text Study at the End of the Twentieth Century* has shaped my thinking about Jewish philosophy, the practice of SR, and the significance of reading as much as any book has.[22] My lack of engagement with and use of Vaughan's dissertation and Levene and Ochs's edited volume does not at all mean that these works are not helpful for understanding the practice of SR. In fact, I recommend readers of this book to seek out those works after reading this book. Because these great works about SR formed and shaped my own arguments concerning the practice of SR, I attempt to write this book without being constantly haunted by Ford's warning about writing about SR.

22. See Ochs and Levene, *Textual Reasonings.*

Part 1

The *Scriptural* Aspect of Scriptural Reasoning

I n Part 1, I focus on the role of scripture in the thinking of two of the founders of SR: David Ford and Peter Ochs. Chapter 1 focuses on Ochs's "return to scripture" and how this return relates to the pragmatism and semiotics of the American philosopher, Charles Sanders Peirce.[1] Chapter 2 explains Ford's claim that theological wisdom can be found in the traditionally sacred texts of Christianity, Judaism, and Islam. I argue that Ford's understanding of theological wisdom relates to the work of the French philosopher, Paul Ricouer.

---

1. I put the phrase "return to scripture" in quotation marks because it's part of the title of Ochs's edited volume, *Return to Scripture in Christianity and Judaism*.

1 ───────────────────────────────

Pragmatism and Semiotics

C. S. Peirce *after* Peter Ochs

A ny account of Scriptural Reasoning must begin with
Peter Ochs's engagement with the American philosopher Charles Sanders Peirce: first, a few words about Peirce's
biography; second, a few words about who Ochs is.[1]

Charles Sanders Peirce (1839–1914) seemed to be an
odd human being. He was the son of the Harvard math-
ematician Benjamin Peirce, and Charles attended Harvard
as both an undergraduate and graduate student. Charles
was a member of the now famous "Metaphysical Club"
where he talked law, politics, and science with William
James, Oliver Wendell Holmes, Chauncey Wright, and others.[2] James and Peirce maintained a deep, if not difficult,
friendship throughout their lives. Charles left his first wife
in order to marry a woman who was working as a prostitute

1. I am in David O'Hara's debt for answering random research
questions I had about Charles Sanders Peirce while writing this chapter, and I am grateful to John Shook for giving me helpful suggestions
for improving this chapter in terms of style and substance.

2. See Menand, *Metaphysical Club*.

when the two met, and he had trouble keeping a job after he divorced his first wife. He taught philosophy at Johns Hopkins University but not for long. He was a bitter person, and this bitterness seemed to have driven him to write and write and write in the rural setting of Milford, Pennsylvania.[3] He struggled with human relationships but changed the course of the history of Western philosophy with his philosophical systems known as pragmatism, semiotics, and three-valued logic. Charles died in 1914.[4]

Personality-wise, Peter Ochs seems worlds away from his favorite philosopher and intellectual hero. Ochs is charitable, gracious, kind—and spends most of his time thinking about community service projects and teaching philosophical method to non-academics. The journalist Jeffrey W. Bailey captures Ochs's personality and spirit quite accurately:

> Ochs is one of the Jewish founders of the Society for Scriptural Reasoning, a professor of Modern Judaic Studies at the University of Virginia, and a primary impetus behind SR's development. At the meeting [that Bailey attended], he [Ochs] talks about the possibilities for an "Abrahamic theo-politics," and the group questions him as to the role Scriptural Reasoning might play. His friendly manner belies an intellectual intensity, and after each of his rapidly-delivered answers, he says to his questioner, "But what do *you* think?" He seems determined to make things conversational, and positively lights up when

3. The Peirce Edition Project projects a total of thirty volumes for publishing all of Peirce's writings: "The Project's long-term aim is to produce a thirty-volume print edition of Peirce's writings" (https://peirce.iupui.edu).

4. Joseph Brent's biography remains both engaging and reliable; see Brent, *Charles Sanders Peirce*.

someone disagrees with him. He talks about his hope that new ways of religious reasoning among people of faith might emerge. "People assume that problems among religious groups arise out of religious differences. So, to bring such groups together, they try to avoid religion altogether and turn to some supposedly shared interest, like economic development," he says. "Our assumption is the opposite: that religious people like each other because they *are* religious. They are moved by piety, discipline, and love of God to pursue similar ends and find solutions."[5]

Ochs earned his undergraduate degree in anthropology and his PhD in philosophy from Yale University, with an additional master's degrees from the Jewish Theological Seminary in New York City. Ochs taught at Colgate University in New York and Drew University in New Jersey before becoming the Edgar Bronfmann Chair of Modern Judaic Studies at the University of Virginia (UVa).

In this first chapter, I explain technical theories in non-technical ways—to the best of my ability. The goal of this chapter concerns the ways in which Ochs employs and engages with the thought of C. S. Peirce resulting in making Peirce's pragmatism and semiotics the most obvious foundations for the practice of Scriptural Reasoning.[6] The thesis statement of this chapter is that Ochs's use of Peirce's philosophy for describing and developing SR leads

5. Bailey, "New Models for Religion in Public," 36.

6. I do not mean "foundations" in the sense of foundationalism. I fought the battle of whether Ochs is a foundationalist in a problematic way, and I argue that he is not. For the case that Ochs has a problematic foundationalism, see Lamberth's "Assessing Peter Ochs through *Peirce, Pragmatism, and the Logic of Scripture*," 459–67; for my response to Lamberth, see Goodson, *Narrative Theology and the Hermeneutical Virtues*, ch. 5.

to an unresolved tension within the practice of SR: pragmatism vs. semiotics.

Why Scripture?

It is not typical for a philosopher like Ochs to take such an interest in scripture—the canonical books of the Jewish, Christian, and Muslim traditions. I detect two motivations for Ochs's interest in scripture: one based upon his reading of Peirce's pragmatism and another based upon his commitment to Judaism. These come together in his formulation(s) for the practice of SR.

Why Scripture? The Pragmatist Answer

Peirce, Pragmatism, and the Logic of Scripture remains Ochs's most important book. In that book, Ochs outlines three ways in which Peirce's philosophy leads philosophy and philosophers back to the Christian Scriptures. First, what Ochs calls "the agency of scripture" in Peirce's thinking: "Peirce calls graph writing 'scripture,' as in 'scribing a graph,' and names the two persons who collaborate on the graph the *graphist* and the *interpreter*."[7] Before Peirce arrives at the *particularity of Christian Scripture*, he thinks through the *general meaning of the word "Scripture"*: a graph inscribed *by* someone and *for* someone else.[8]

Second, Peirce envisioned a philosophical community analogous to the ecclesial community—which Peirce called "the great catholic church."[9] Like the "great catholic church," according to Ochs, Peirce sought for the

7. Ochs, *PPLS*, 207.

8. See Ochs, *PPLS*, 207.

9. Peirce, "What Is Christian Faith?," 443.

philosophical community to make their scripture Scripture.[10] Peirce envisioned, in Ochs's words, certain

> communities of philosophers who identify their
> scripture with Scripture, or the Bible. They read
> Scripture as the prototypical narrative of how
> certain musers . . . were stimulated by their
> observations of human suffering to undertake
> corrective-and-diagrammatic inquiries that ter-
> minate . . . in the musers' dialogues with God.[11]

This represents Peirce's move from the general meaning of scripture to the particular use of Christian Scripture. Communities need texts that function as graphs, in Peirce's sense of the word. For a certain community of philosophers, the Christian canon ought to have this function or play this role. The reason that Christian Scriptures should have this function or play this role concerns how they provide narratives that relate human suffering to "dialogues with God."[12]

Within philosophy, identifying human suffering belongs to the areas of aesthetics (Aristotle's *Poetics*) and/ or ethics (Aristotle's *Nichomachean Ethics*) while dialogues with God belong to ethics (Plato's *Euthyphro*) and/ or the philosophy of religion (Plato's *Laws*). The works in parenthesis pinpoint foundational texts for how human suffering relates to the study of aesthetics and ethics and how dialogues with God relates to the study of ethics and philosophy of religion.[13] The Christian Bible models how all of these connect to each other and provides an object of study that brings together philosophers interested in

10. See Ochs, *PPLS*, 287.

11. Ochs, *PPLS*, 287.

12. See Ochs, *PPLS*, 287.

13. See Ochs, *PPLS*, 287.

the relationship between human suffering, speaking about God, and talking to God.[14]

Third, Peirce moves beyond the claim that the Christian Bible serves as merely a model. According to Ochs, Peirce "illustrates how a philosopher actually graphs God's attributes . . . [and] illustrates how *communities of scriptural philosophers* actually graph God's attributes of compassion-and-correction."[15] The Christian Scriptures offer a particular graph of God's attributes, and Ochs's words of compassion and correction can be replaced with a plethora of synonyms. From my own tradition of Lutheranism, we would say Law (correction) and Gospel (compassion). Others might substitute love and justice: love for compassion and justice for correction. Still others might see compassion as equivalent to the categories of grace or mercy, whereas correction is equivalent to judgment and wrath. The point is that Ochs seems right about this in relation to how God is presented—how the New Testament authors graph their dialogues with God—in the Christian Scriptures.[16] For Peirce, certain communities of philosophers ought to take these divine attributes as normative for their enquiries into aesthetics, ethics, and the philosophy of religion.

What does this mean for SR? Straightforwardly, it means that Ochs's invention of the practice of SR became his way to create a philosophical community of enquirers who take the New Testament—and added to the New Testament the Tanakh and the Qur'an—as normative for conversations concerning aesthetics, ethics, and the philosophy

14. For a helpful analysis concerning the differences between how philosophers speak about God and how Christian theologians speak about God, see Long, *Speaking of God*.

15. Ochs, *PPLS*, 290.

16. See Ochs, *PPLS*, 287.

of religion.[17] While not all scriptural reasoners are trained

17. How does Ochs do this in his own writing (independent from being in a SR group with Ochs)? For one instance, see my analysis of Ochs's interpretation of Matthew 7 in Goodson, *Introducing Prophetic Pragmatism*, 123–33. For another instance, I quote Ochs's explicit use of Peirce's doctrine of irremediable vagueness for interpreting Exodus 3: "The divine discourses of scripture and prayer introduce a vocabulary that by definition exceeds the limits of human comprehension. In Charles Peirce's logical terms, each name of God is irremediably vague. This means that each name is a deictic sign that points directly and forcefully to the reality and presence of God . . . but also discloses something of this God, introducing this something into our lives and understanding so that the naming changes what we know as well as reinforcing the limited character of all that we know.

In the scriptural account of Exodus . . . God discloses such names as *ehyeh imach*, 'I will be with you,' or *ehyeh asher ehyeh*, 'I will be what I will be,' or *yhvh* (the unspeakable name). . . . For the romantic or cataphatic postliberal, these names all imply the deictic You, but they are not reducible to it alone. They add bits of information about the God and God's relation to creation and to us. Indeed, as both postmodern and postliberal thinkers would argue, we cannot fully capture any of this information in discrete sentences of our natural language. In Peirce's terms again, the information is introduced vaguely. This does not mean, however, that sentences of natural language are not useful means of delivering this vague information to us, or clarifying or extending it; it is simply a warning against self-satisfied or idolatrous employment of any single set of natural language sentences or descriptions.

It is worthwhile to learn . . . that 'God may be with me,' provided I bear in mind that the learning is never exhausted by any single take I may have on what that phrase means. This caution is no ground for radical skepticism, however, for it should apply as well to ways we come to know other human beings or perhaps all other things. Say, for example, that I know you as 'my friend' or 'that fast runner.' Yes, these attributions are much less vague than those we make of God, but they are vague nonetheless: we may understand them differently at different times and, to be sure, we may have reason to change them altogether at different times. In sum, theological language carries with it special instructions about how to use it, and it certainly cannot be used as if it were equivalent to any given set of natural language conventions. But this is to say no more than that theological

as philosophers, all scriptural reasoners participate in this Peircean-inspired philosophical community that bases itself on how God is graphed through scripture.

In his book, *C. S. Peirce and the Nested Continua Model of Religious Interpretation*, Gary Slater puts into two sentences the Peircean significance of Scripture for Ochs:

> Hence the reference to *Scriptural* Reasoning . . . bears on two distinctive features of Ochs's work: the centrality of the text, and the meaning of texts in relation to various readerships. . . . As for the meaning of the term "reasoning" in Scriptural Reasoning, this refers to the structures of interpretation that are revealed when the plain sense of Scripture *itself* appears unable to perform its task of repairing everyday problems.[18]

Slater identifies the significance of both the *scriptural* and the *reasoning* aspect of Ochs's Scriptural Reasoning project: scriptural, because of the centrality of the scriptural text and the semiotic relation of the scriptural text to various communities of readers; reasoning, because of "the structures of interpretation that are revealed" when performing the "task of repairing everyday problems."[19]

Why Scripture? The Jewish Answer

It might seem obvious to say that Ochs's commitment to Judaism leads him to take Scripture seriously, but the so-called

language is a special language, as are the languages of mathematics, physics, and poetry, or even how to play Monopoly. It takes education to know how to use any such language, and rules of vagueness and probability are appropriate features of any special language. No need, then, for radical skepticism, just for appropriate wisdom." Ochs, "Pragmatic Cataphasis," §2.3.

18. Slater, *C. S. Peirce and the Nested Continua Model*, 123.

19. See Slater, *C. S. Peirce and the Nested Continua Model*, 123.

postliberal part of Ochs's thinking means that he finds he must "return to Scripture" after its "eclipse" within Jewish philosophy and Judaism.[20] In order to avoid the fallacy of hasty generalization, in this section I will talk about Jewish philosophy specifically rather than Judaism in general. Ochs's "An Introduction to Postcritical Scriptural Interpretation" outlines his own Jewish "return to Scripture."[21]

Ochs utilizes Hans Frei's diagnoses of how modern philosophy slowly "eclipsed" biblical narratives.[22] Within modern philosophy, Frei blames Baruch Spinoza, John Locke, and others.[23] Ochs seems agreeable to this diagnosis. Frei emphasizes modern philosophy's impact on Christian theology, and Ochs makes the same claim for Jewish philosophy. Ochs writes, for instance, "the argument of both Jewish and Christian postcritical interpreters is that modern scholars have reduced biblical interpretation to the terms of a dyadic semiotic that lacks warrant in the biblical texts."[24] This reduction led to making the Jewish Scriptures—the Tanakh—so unhelpful and uninteresting that, within Jewish philosophy, it became a hurdle to overcome rather than a source of wisdom to continually draw from.

This "return to Scripture" involves what I mean by the terms postliberal and postliberalism.[25] By "returning to Scripture" after the liberalism of modernity, which slowly "eclipses" the narratives of the Jewish and Christian Scriptures, postliberalism in this context does not have to mean anti-liberalism or anti-modernity but, rather, a particular

20. See Ochs, PSI, 3–53.

21. See Ochs, PSI, 3–53.

22. See Frei, *Eclipse of Biblical Narrative*, 1-16.

23. See Goodson, *Narrative Theology and the Hermeneutical Virtues*, chs. 1–4.

24. Ochs, PSI, 38.

25. See Ochs, PSI, 3–53.

failure or result of liberalism within modernity which makes biblical narratives so unhelpful and uninteresting that both citizens and scholars lose a significant source of wisdom for their everyday lives and scholarly pursuits.[26] Ochs seeks his contribution to the tradition of Jewish philosophy to serve as a "return to Scripture" in relation to the tendency within Jewish philosophy, after Spinoza, to take a reductive—and, therefore, problematic—approach to the Tanakh.[27]

Peirce, Hermeneutics, and Semiotics

What does it mean to treat Peirce's semiotics as a theory of interpretation (i.e., hermeneutics)? I navigate Ochs's understanding and use of Peirce's semiotics as a hermeneutic in relation to other treatments of Peirce's semiotics as a theory of interpretation. Like Ochs, other scholars connect Peirce's semiotics with a hermeneutics of Scripture. Some scholars, however, see in Peirce's semiotics a more general hermeneutic. What Ochs sees in Peirce's work—the potential for a hermeneutic that requires communal reading—other

26. After conversations with David Dault, Marianne Moyaert, and Matthew Vaughan, I decided to write this book without making the case that SR is necessarily a postliberal practice—in the sense of postliberalism as a theological method developed by and found in the "Yale school of theology." They convinced me that the postliberalism of the "Yale school of theology" might be present in Ochs's thinking about SR but severely limits the inclusiveness and scope of the practice of SR. Both Dault and Moyaert have written on this problem: see Dault, "Catholic Reasoning and Reading Across Traditions," 46–61; Moyaert, "Scriptural Reasoning as Inter-Religious Dialogue," 64–86. Gary Slater's take on the role of postliberalism in Ochs's thinking, however, seems more modest and less problematic: "Reflecting its postliberal influence, the sources for guidance in Scriptural Reasoning lie in its communal, historically situated traditions." Slater, *C. S. Peirce and the Nested Continua Model*, 123.

27. See Ochs, PSI, 3-53.

Peirce scholars see as well. In what follows, I outline the ways in which three other thinkers see in Peirce's semiotics a theory of interpretation: the famous Italian novelist and philosopher Umberto Eco, literary theorist William Elford Rogers, and American philosopher Robert Corrington (Ochs's former colleague at Drew University). This section gives readers a stronger sense of Peirce's semiotics than what I have offered thus far in this chapter.

Scriptural Reasoning *after* Umberto Eco

Umberto Eco might be famous for writing novels such as *Foucault's Pendulum* and *The Name of the Rose*, but he also writes as a scholar of Charles Sanders Peirce's philosophy. I focus on one of his books where Peirce is the main intellectual character: *The Limits of Interpretation*. Although he never references the practice of Scriptural Reasoning, his development of Peirce's semiotics as a kind of hermeneutics resembles the role of Peirce's philosophy in SR.

In Peirce's semiotics, Eco finds an interpretation theory that avoids particular problems within both medieval and modern theories of interpretation. I reconstruct his argument in five points. First, Eco claims, "any act of interpretation is a dialectic between openness and form, initiative on the part of the interpreter and contextual pressure."[28] Medieval theories of interpretation tend to prioritize "form" over "openness" whereas modern theories of interpretation tend to prioritize "openness" over "form."[29] Peirce's semiotics requires both: "a dialectic between openness and form."[30]

28. Eco, *Limits of Interpretation*, 21.

29. Eco, *Limits of Interpretation*, 21.

30. Eco, *Limits of Interpretation*, 21.

This "dialectic between openness and form" becomes a necessary feature of SR, where participants must be open to the text and to other interpretations of those texts.[31] Additionally, SR only works if the interpretations offered have a substantial form to them. Within SR, being open to the text and to others does not mean being 'nice' to other participants. It means, instead, that participants need to articulate substantial interpretations that are received by others with a kind of openness that leads to in-depth engagements with one another rather than mere agreement.

Second, Eco identifies problems he sees in both medieval and modern theories of interpretation. He writes,

> Medieval interpreters were wrong in taking the world as a univocal text; modern interpreters are wrong in taking every text as an unshaped world. Texts are the human way to reduce the world to a manageable format, open to an intersubjective interpretive discourse. Which means that, when symbols are inserted into a text, there is . . . no way to decide which interpretation is the "good" one, but it is still possible to decide, on the basis of the context, which one is due, not to an effort of understanding "that" text, but rather to a hallucinatory response on the part of the addressee.[32]

The problem with medieval theories of interpretation concerns how they encourage a singular meaning, both within texts and within the world. The problem with modern theories of interpretation involves an assumption of humanism: texts remain unformed or unshaped until human reason molds them.

31. The phrase in quotation marks comes from Eco, *Limits of Interpretation*, 21.

32. Eco, *Limits of Interpretation*, 21.

Peirce's semiotics ought to be understood as a system that offers the ability to affirm (a) texts do have some inherent meaning; (b) the meaning of texts is not univocal, and interpreters give texts multiple meanings in addition to the inherent meaning; and (c) human rationality contributes to the meaning of texts and even shapes certain texts, but this process is best described as *semiotic* precisely because human reason shapes texts while texts simultaneously shape human reason as well. For Peirce, semiosis requires this *constant reciprocity*.

In the context of the practice of SR, this means that engagements around scriptural passages ought to involve an exercise of constant questioning. Participant A offers an interpretation about Genesis 1:1; this interpretation might add to the meaning of Genesis 1:1, or it might be a "hallucinatory response" to the sense of Genesis 1; participant B, therefore, raises a question or set of questions that helps both participant A and the other participants in the SR study group determine if said interpretation ought to be judged as contributory or hallucinatory—not in line with the sense of Genesis 1.[33] Yes, our interpretations add and contribute to the meaning of Genesis 1:1; the sense of Genesis 1:1 also forms, informs, and shapes the ways in which our rational faculty gains the ability to even offer an interpretation of Genesis 1:1. This is what Peircean *constant reciprocity* looks like within SR.

Third, Eco learns from Peirce's semiotics what it means to come to an agreement about the meaning of a text. He writes,

> [T]o reach an agreement about the nature of a
> given text does not mean either (a) that the inter-
> preters must trace back to the original intention

33. The phrase in quotation marks comes from Eco, *Limits of Interpretation*, 21.

> of the author or (b) that such a text must have
> a unique and final meaning. There are "open"
> texts that support multiple interpretations, and
> any common agreement about them ought to
> concern . . . their open nature and the textual
> strategies that make them work that way.[34]

Medieval theories of interpretation regard agreement about the meaning of texts as the goal of interpretation whereas modern theories of interpretation aim for making texts *agree with* human rationality. According to Eco, Peirce's semiotics shifts both of these hermeneutical goals. Yes, we can reach agreement about texts; the agreement, however, does not concern the meaning of texts but "their open nature."[35] Yes, human rationality relates to interpreting texts. Texts, however, do not need to be read to conform to human rationality; rather, human rationality aids and instructs us in learning how to "support multiple interpretations" of those texts.[36]

Eco's development of Peirce's semiotics as a theory of interpretation speaks to a difficulty within SR that, sometimes, makes both conservatives and liberals skeptical of the practice.[37] Conservatives tend to avoid or critique the practice of SR because of the need for agreement, within the practice of SR, about the openness of scriptural passages. Usually, SR practitioners respond to this criticism by saying: *only during the practice of SR do we need to make this agreement.*[38] In other words, SR asks of participants only

34. Eco, *Limits of Interpretation*, 41.

35. Eco, *Limits of Interpretation*, 41.

36. See Eco, *Limits of Interpretation*, 41.

37. I use these labels for heuristic purposes—my intent does not involve perpetuating a bad and unhelpful binary that negatively impacts all of us on a daily basis.

38. This represents one of those rules for SR, mentioned in the

for a type of pretend-agreement about the openness of texts for the purpose of SR sessions. Liberals tend to be annoyed by the practice of SR because strict SR practitioners bluntly challenge any and all interpretations of scriptural passages that make those passages sound modern or progressive. In other words, some SR practitioners see it as their mission to constantly and directly challenge the modern (in Eco's sense of the word) tendency of aiming to make texts agree with the tenets of human rationality.

Fourth, Eco introduces the role of Peirce's concept of musement in his semiotics. Eco writes,

> [E]ven though the interpreters cannot decide which interpretation is the privileged one, they can agree on the fact that certain interpretations are not contextually legitimated. Thus, even though using a text as a playground for imple-menting unlimited semiosis, they can agree that at certain moments the "play of musement" can transitorily stop by producing a consensual judgment.[39]

Eco emphasizes how texts impact readers. In Peirce's semi-otics, texts read readers as much as readers read texts! This reciprocity between reading texts and being read by texts is how Eco applies Pierce's recommendation of playful thinking—musement—to the process of interpretation. Readers should allow themselves to be playful with texts, and this playfulness occurs in the process of reading texts and being read by texts.

Semiosis encourages and requires musement as a means to "producing a consensual judgment."[40] According to SR practitioners and theorists, the practice of SR does not

introduction, that arises organically within the argument.

39. Eco, *Limits of Interpretation*, 41–42.

40. Eco, *Limits of Interpretation*, 42.

lead to consensus in judgments about the meaning of texts. Within SR, therefore, Peircean musement is not treated as a means to "producing a consensual judgment."[41] In this book, what is meant by musement or playfulness relates to one of Eco's points but differs from another one of his points: *playfulness involves the process of being read by texts while reading those texts with others,* but it does not include "producing a consensual judgment."[42] Perhaps the best description that I can give of SR is: *SR sessions provide "a playground for implementing [this] unlimited semiosis."*[43] In this sense, SR is the philosopher's playground.

Eco's fifth and final point captures an aspect of SR that can be taken as both liberating yet frustrating. In Eco's words: "it is very difficult to decide whether a given interpretation is a good one, [but] it is . . . always possible to decide whether it is a bad one."[44] This certainly describes SR in the sense that there are no agreed upon standards of judgment within SR: Would an interpretation be judged as 'good' because it conforms to either doctrines within a particular religious tradition or methods within academic biblical studies? SR allows neither of these to function as absolute standards. If an interpretation seems to make no sense in relation to the scriptural passage that everyone has in front of them, then such an interpretation can be deemed as 'bad' within the conversational engagements nurtured by SR. Within SR, participants can determine 'bad' interpretations; 'good' interpretations, however, cannot be judged as such. This point relates to the post-metaphysical methodology of SR, which I develop more in chapters 5 and 8.

41. Eco, *Limits of Interpretation*, 42.

42. Eco, *Limits of Interpretation*, 42.

43. Eco, *Limits of Interpretation*, 42. Emphasis added.

44. Eco, *Limits of Interpretation*, 42.

Although Eco does not connect Peirce's semiotics with interpreting sacred texts, I conclude that his development of Peirce's semiotics as a theory of interpretation offers helpful insights for better understanding the practice of SR and how SR practitioners engage with scriptural passages. At the very least, Eco gives us ways in which Peirce's semiotics—and SR as a practice following Peirce's semiotics—can be understood as an alternative to both medieval and modern theories of interpretation. Eco's development of Peirce's semiotics into a theory of interpretation demonstrates that Ochs's use of Peirce as the foundational thinker for the practice of SR comes with merit and precedence.

Scriptural Reasoning *after* William Rogers

William Rogers makes Peirce the intellectual hero of his book on "textual hermeneutics as an ascetic discipline."[45] Rogers focuses on the textuality of Peirce's semiotics. Rogers's argument helps identify both the communal-aspect and future-orientation of SR, and SR can be described as an "ascetic discipline" on the Peircean terms that Rogers uses to develop that phrase.[46]

First, Rogers's use of the phrase "ascetic discipline" means that interpretation should be neither seen nor understood as an individual practice.[47] A Peircean-based hermeneutics becomes an ascetic discipline in the sense that interpretation always involves the priority of a community over individual rationality.[48]

My claim is that SR puts into practice this notion of ascetic discipline by ensuring that scriptural passages are

45. See Rogers, *Interpreting Interpretation*, 139–77.

46. See Rogers, *Interpreting Interpretation*, 139–77.

47. See Rogers, *Interpreting Interpretation*, 139–77.

48. See Rogers, *Interpreting Interpretation*, 139–77.

always read together, within community, so that the individual rationality of a singular person does not take precedence within the process of interpretation.[49] When SR practitioners and theorists claim that no singular person can act as an authority within a SR session, it is meant to signal this priority of community over individual rationality.

Second, Rogers compares Peirce's semiotics with the practice of "textual interpretation" within literary studies.[50] He writes,

> Peirce talks about the explanation that necessarily belongs to every sign. There is "some explanation or argument or other context, showing how—upon what system or for what reason— the Sign represents the Object." . . . In textual interpretation the interpretive statement is a sign of—that is, stands for—the text. . . . Peirce suggests that there is some explicit or implicit set of interconnected rules . . . for moving from the significant features of the text to the interpretive statement. I can "argue for" or "support" my interpretation, in other words, by explaining the principles on which I have connected the features of the text to the features of my interpretive statement. This system of rules and principles is what I am calling the *interpretive system*. To apply an interpretive system means precisely to take something into the chain of significance, to take it as a sign, or as a *word* in the broad sense that Peirce uses when he says that the word or sign a person uses *is* the person.[51]

---

49. On the phrase in quotation marks, see Rogers, *Interpreting Interpretation*, 139–77.

50. See Rogers, *Interpreting Interpretation*, 20.

51. Rogers, *Interpreting Interpretation*, 20–21.

In Peirce's argument for "the explanation that necessarily belongs to every sign," Rogers finds a set of rules for getting from "significant features of the text" to an "interpretive statement."[52] An "*interpretive system*" can be referenced that enables an interpreter of a text to defend their particular interpretation of that text with an explanation of rules for interpretation.[53] To reference this "*interpretive system*" for defending a particular interpretation is to envelop a sign or a word into a system of signs and words.[54]

What Rogers calls "the interpretive system" becomes one way to describe the conversational dynamics within the practice of SR. To transfer Rogers's words to what a SR session looks like: SR participants "'argue for' or 'support' [their] interpretation . . . by explaining the principles on which [they] have connected the features of the text to the features of [their] interpretive statement."[55] At its most basic, SR simply is the performance and practice of this system articulated by Rogers.

Third, Rogers emphasizes the future-orientation of Peirce's interpretation theory. He writes,

> By Peirce's theory of semiosis, interpreting means connecting one sign (or chain of signs) with another, according to some principle or set of principles. That is, I produce an interpretive statement about a text according to some interpretive system. But by the infinitely replicative nature of semiosis, my interpretive statement is now susceptible to being taken up in another interpretive statement, and so on. In fact, according to Peirce, my interpretive statement is only

52. Rogers, *Interpreting Interpretation*, 20.

53. See Rogers, *Interpreting Interpretation*, 21.

54. See Rogers, *Interpreting Interpretation*, 21.

55. Rogers, *Interpreting Interpretation*, 20.

> virtually a sign of the text. It can become a sign
> only insofar as it has the potential to be taken
> up in an infinitely self-replicating chain of signs
> that directs itself toward the perfected knowl-
> edge of an indefinitely future community.[56]

Because the process of semiotics—called semiosis—is "infinitely replicative," interpretive statements are enveloped into
other interpretive statements that are enveloped into other
interpretive statements and so on.[57] This is all an interpretive statement can do for Peirce: become a sign of the text
and infinitely replicate itself. This "infinitely self-replicating
chain of signs" involves a teleological drive toward a definite
"future community."[58] This "future community," for Peirce,
is the time and place where knowledge gets "perfected."[59]
The *telos* of Peirce's semiotics is that of "perfected knowledge" in a "future community."[60]

Peter Ochs thinks of SR groups as embodying and
signifying—not in full but in part—this Peircean notion
of a perfected future community. The histories of relations
between Christians, Jews, and Muslims has been determined by conflict and violence. SR repairs these historical relationships—not only by putting Jews, Muslims, and
Christians in the same room together for a definite period
of time—but also by turning members of these traditions
into a particular and peculiar kind of community: a community of scriptural interpreters engaged in a semiotic
process. *If Eco's take on Peirce's hermeneutics offers a sense
of the playful side of SR, then Rogers's development of Peirce's
hermeneutics provides a sense of the pragmatist side of SR:*

56. Rogers, *Interpreting Interpretation*, 166.

57. See Rogers, *Interpreting Interpretation*, 166.

58. Rogers, *Interpreting Interpretation*, 166.

59. Rogers, *Interpreting Interpretation*, 166.

60. Rogers, *Interpreting Interpretation*, 166.

SR's definite end concerns turning traditionally broken relationships into a healed community of Christians, Jews, and Muslims. Of course, Rogers does not put it in these Abrahamic terms. Rogers's emphasis on the future-orientation of Peirce's interpretation theory aligns with and correlates to Ochs's description of SR as a peace-making activity working toward a perfected Abrahamic communi-ty.[61] Within this book, what I mean by the *pragmatist* and *purposeful* side of SR concerns this insight from Rogers that a Peircean interpretation theory involves a teleological drive toward a definite "future community."[62]

Peirce's Hermeneutics and Semiotics at Drew University

Prior to 1997, both Robert Corrington and Peter Ochs were professors at Drew University in Madison, New Jersey.[63] In 1997, Ochs moved to UVa; Corrington remained at Drew until his retirement in January 2020. Both Corrington and Ochs spent time developing Peirce's semiotics into a theory of interpretation, and I compare and contrast their develop-ments on this question.

First, Peirce's semiotics leads to a communal herme-neutic. Corrington claims, "Peirce's semiotics gave him the tools for developing a hermeneutics and for showing its relation to the community of interpreters. Initially we can define semiotics as the systematic study of those items

61. See Geddes, "Peacemaking among the Abrahamic Faiths," 90–102.

62. Rogers, *Interpreting Interpretation*, 166.

63. In the spirit of Gary Slater's argument that there is a "Charlot-tesville Pragmatism" between Ochs and Rorty (see Slater, "Charlot-tesville Pragmatism"), perhaps we could consider this section the beginning of the development of a Drew Pragmatism between Cor-rington and Ochs.

in experience known as signs."[64] Corrington defines semiotics as the study of what is found "in experience known as signs."[65] According to Corrington, "Peirce . . . restricted the realm of signs to the realm of thought. That is, he argued that all thought must exist in signs, but that which lies outside of thought need not be a sign."[66] All thinking, for Peirce, is semiotic in the sense that in order for thought to be thought it necessarily involves signs. This relates to hermeneutics because it involves a "community of interpreters"—a community that attempts to offer a system for interpreting "experience."[67]

Second, knowledge of the self requires an act of interpretation. In Corrington's words: "A sign refers to an object (denotation) in some way (connotation) and to some thought (interpretant)"—which means, "when we look into ourselves we must follow this general threefold pattern. We see our self in some respect, and our seeing produces an interpretant or thought about the self."[68] The self is only intelligible within a triadic relationship: an unexamined self, an experience of the self, and an interpretation or thought produced about the self. Therefore, even to know one's self requires interpretation: to know one's self involves being in an interpretive relationship with oneself. An interpretation of oneself has to be produced in order for there to be a conception or understanding of the self at all.

Third, signs are not for the sake of themselves but rather for the interpreter to interpret. Corrington claims, "Signs . . . are always signs for someone, namely, an interpreter. The interpreter has the function of interpreting

64. Corrington, *Community of Interpreters*, 2.

65. Corrington, *Community of Interpreters*, 2.

66. Corrington, *Community of Interpreters*, 2.

67. See Corrington, *Community of Interpreters*, 2.

68. Corrington, *Community of Interpreters*, 11.

the given sign to another. Thus we can see how signs can be understood only within the complex structures of a community."[69] Semiotics not only requires *interpretation* but also requires *interpreters*; in Peirce's semiotics, *interpretation* always involves an *interpreter*. Semiotics does not allow for an individuated interpreter but, rather, requires a complex communal structure of interpreters. Interpretation takes place with other interpreters in this complex communal structure.

Fourth, Corrington contrasts Peirce's semiotics with Friedrich Schleiermacher's hermeneutics. He writes,

> Peirce went beyond the earlier hermeneutic formulation of Schleiermacher by insisting that the expressions of language do not reveal a substantive self-consciousness with one determinate, if evolving nature. We do not necessarily know the "author better than he knew himself," as it is unclear just what ontological status the self would have. Peirce . . . came to see the self in semiotic terms and thus raised the problem of self-identity to new levels of complexity and interest. Yet, like Schleiermacher, [Peirce] believed that our external expressions are a fair indication of our internal nature, however complex that nature may be.[70]

Corrington's move here contains similarities with Eco's argument that Peirce's semiotics differ from modern theories of interpretation.

The German philosopher and theologian Friedrich Schleiermacher (1768–1834) famously argues that, in the hermeneutic process, an interpreter of a text is able to come

---

69. Corrington, *Community of Interpreters*, 14.
70. Corrington, *Community of Interpreters*, 14.

to know the author better than the author knew themself.[71] Peirce's semiotics question such a claim—not because Peirce thinks it wrong but, rather, because it lacks real substance. Interpreters come to know the mind of the author only through the interpretive process. The author comes to know themself the same way that others come to know them: through the process of interpretation. Both Peirce and Schleiermacher agree that interpretation is required for knowledge, which involves the claim that there is no internal privileged access that a person has to themself.

Lastly, concerning Corrington's interpretation of Peirce, the scientific community serves as the best model for what Peirce means by *communal* in his semiotics. Corrington explains,

> Knowledge, which itself is based on signs, can be won only when the individual identifies with the life of the community. For Peirce, the ideal model for the perfect community is the community of science. The scientific community is a self-corrective domain of free inquiry into the semiotic structures of objects and events. The community renews itself by placing all inferences under the skeptical eye of the researchers, who are dedicated to the search for counterexamples. The community has the teleological drive toward the ideal future in which scientific knowledge is secure and based on general metaphysical principles such as that of *agape-ism*.[72]

The scientific community serves as the ideal community and the ideal model for communal-thinking because it is "self-corrective" and continually "renews itself" through

71. See Schleiermacher, *Hermeneutics and Criticism*.

72. Corrington, *Community of Interpreters*, 15.

"the skeptical eye of . . . researchers."[73] Also, the scientific community is "teleological" in that it thinks *forward* to an "ideal future" when "scientific knowledge is secure" and has proper "metaphysical principles" in place.[74] Therefore, both the scientific community and the teleological drive toward the future are necessary parts of Peirce's semiotics because they serve as Peirce's ideals in his semiotics.

Corrington's interpretation of Peirce offers a good picture of what a theory of interpretation looks like based upon the combination of Peirce's philosophy of science, pragmatism, and semiotics. According to Corrington, Peirce's semiotics involves the necessity of interpretation for thought and understanding, as well for knowledge of the self. Corrington does not focus on the interpretation of *texts* per se but, rather, how semiotics can be understood as an *interpretive process*. The ideals of this interpretive process involve the scientific community as a model for communal interpretation and the teleological drive toward the future.

The similarity between Corrington and Ochs is that both make Peirce's philosophy of science necessary for understanding Peirce's pragmatism and semiotics. Peirce's semiotics involves *textuality*, according to Ochs, because of the emphasis on the limits of knowing a metaphysical reality "beyond the experimental result."[75] For Ochs, this conviction formed in the laboratory carries over as a conviction about how texts *work*. Peirce does not deny a metaphysical reality; Peirce denies how much individual knowers can know reality. Likewise with reading texts: In reading texts, a careful reader does not necessarily deny a metaphysical reality outside of the text; rather, a careful (scientific) reader remains within the limitations determined by that

73. Corrington, *Community of Interpreters*, 15.

74. See Corrington, *Community of Interpreters*, 15.

75. Ochs, *PPLS*, 166.

particular text. Because of these limitations, a reader who bases interpretation on experimentalism and logic knows not to go or move beyond the boundaries set by the text. Hence, within SR, participants often say: (a) do not go beyond the words in front of us, or (b) let's not speculate about what seems out of reach for this particular passage.[76] This means that SR asks its participants to read texts as if they are treating those texts on the terms of how a scientist treats her object of study within a scientific laboratory.

However, the difference between Corrington's and Ochs's interpretations of Peirce's philosophy involve what scholars call general hermeneutics versus particular hermeneutics. Whereas Corrington focuses on how Peirce's semiotics is an *interpretive process* in general, Ochs stresses how Peirce's semiotics serves as a *scriptural* or *textual interpretive process* in particular. In other words, Ochs moves from interpretation in general to the interpretation of Scripture in particular.

Ochs recognizes how Peirce bases his pragmatism on Scripture—specifically Jesus's logical rule found in the Gospels (Matthew 7)—and says that Peirce intends for this to function in ways more than mere proof-texting the Bible to persuade an American audience.[77] According to Ochs, Peirce intends for his pragmatism to invite readers to return again and again to the Christian Scriptures for guidance in relation to logic, science, and theology. *As a scholar who primarily studies American Philosophy, I see and think of SR mostly in this vein: as a way to put into practice Peirce's encouragement and recommendation that pragmatists return again and again to the Christian Scriptures for guidance concerning logic, science, and theology.* In this sense, Ochs's Scriptural Reasoning project fills a void within American

76. Both of these tend to serve as rules within most SR groups.

77. See Ochs, *PPLS*, 315–16.

philosophy since the death of Peirce: no practices have developed—within American philosophy—that allow and invite scholars within American philosophy to study, think through, and utilize the Christian Scriptures.

SR qualifies as a Peircean hermeneutic because it involves (a) interpreting within a community (by definition, SR cannot be practiced by an individual alone), (b) teleological hopes for the future (peace-building among members of traditions who have histories of violence toward one another), and (c) turning to Scripture for guidance and wisdom in relation to logic, science, and theology (SR as a practice for cultivating wisdom will be developed in the next chapter).

Scripture in the Practice of Scriptural Reasoning

Oftentimes, when we hear the phrase "interpreting Scripture," we think of it as an individual activity. In the previous section, however, we learned Peirce thinks of reading as a communal activity. This insight gives us a sense of how a scholar of Peirce's philosophy, like Ochs, might invent a practice of reading together. Ochs calls this Peircean practice Scriptural Reasoning.

Again, why Scripture? This is the question I hear most when talking to people about the practice of Scriptural Reasoning. In his most recent book, *Religion without Violence: The Philosophy and Practice of Scriptural Reasoning*, Ochs attempts a one-sentence answer to this question: "Scriptural Reasoning acquires its name from a conspicuous practice in Abrahamic traditions of turning to scriptural texts as a primary means of accessing the hearth of a given religious community."[78] Therefore, the most basic answer to the

78. Ochs, *RWV*, 18.

question, "Why Scripture?" involves the recognition that to understand religious believers and communities, at some point one has to read and study the canon or texts that those believers and communities take as authoritative.

Ochs also perceives the role of Scripture within SR as radically different than how two groups of people tend to view Scripture. On the one hand, religious believers tend to view Scripture as *their* authoritative text. In relation to how religious believers view Scripture, the practice of Scriptural Reasoning requires *sharing* Scripture—making *my* texts available to the religious other—and *receiving* other texts as equally authoritative. In the conclusion to this book, I use the Kantian universalization test as a rule within SR for achieving what Ochs means by this.

Academics, on the other hand, tend to view Scripture as requiring a specific—sometimes singular—set of tools for interpretation. In relation to how academics treat Scripture, the practice of Scriptural Reasoning allows the logic and meaning of Scripture to break out of academic limitations and restrictions often put on it. In terms of orientation, religious believers can maintain the view that their Scriptures are *their* Scriptures but must learn how to share their Scripture and receive authoritative sacred texts from other religious traditions. In terms of the skills involved for interpreting Scripture, academic tools can be used but only alongside a plethora of other ways of interpreting, reading, and studying the canons of religious traditions.

Ochs is not alone in these judgments concerning how both academics and religious believers treat Scripture. Ochs's friend, Stanley Hauerwas, uses the metaphor of Scripture being leashed by both academics and religious believers—which results in limiting what traditional sacred texts can say to us today. Indeed, he titles his book *Unleashing the Scripture: Freeing the Bible from Captivity to America.* Hauerwas argues that religious believers put a leash on Scripture when they emphasize *individual interpretation* and *possession of* canonical texts, and he claims that academics put a leash on Scripture with their reductive and strict methodologies for how to interpret these ancient texts. Hauerwas and Ochs share in the diagnosis of the problems of how Scripture gets treated by both academics and religious believers, and Ochs's Scriptural Reasoning project puts into practice constructive ways to unleash the scriptures of the Abrahamic traditions.

Conclusion

In Ochs's reflections on SR, we find a real Peircean struggle between pragmatism and semiotics. On the one hand, Ochs wants to promise certain consequences of what the practice of SR will lead to for individual participants. On the other hand, such promises violate the emphasis on Scripture—individual passages for study—and the overall justification for SR: SR is a practice that is good in itself and not because it serves particular ends.[79] Ochs's struggle displays and repeats two key features of Peirce's own philosophy: the *pragmatist* emphasis on potential conceptual and practical consequences[80] vs. the encouragement of playfulness within thinking—especially within the philosophy of religion and theological reasoning—that captures Peirce's *semiotics*.[81] In other words, when reflecting upon SR, Ochs struggles between the playfulness of Peirce's semiotics vs. the purposefulness of Peirce's pragmatism. This

79. See the epigraph from Plato's *Republic*: Ochs thinks of SR in terms of Glaucon's "second class of goods"!

80. See Peirce, "How to Make Our Ideas Clear," 124–41.

81. See Peirce, "Neglected Argument for the Reality of God," 434–50.

tension has created and led to many fruitful and significant disagreements within the Society of Scriptural Reasoning concerning what SR is mostly about.[82]

In terms of the relationship between playfulness, Scripture, and semiotics in Ochs's reflections on SR, I argue that Ochs rightfully claims the "*Scriptural text is the primary teacher*"[83] within the practice of SR. When the "Scriptural text [becomes] the primary teacher" during the practice of SR,[84] then "Scripture and reader meet each other at comparable depths."[85] When I say that the pragmatist side violates the emphasis on Scripture and the significance of individual passages for study for SR, I mean that the pragmatist side potentially distracts us from achieving this depth.

It seems to me that Ochs talks about this depth by employing three different vocabularies, all of which make comparable points and offer similar distinctions:

> From Peirce's Pragmatism: Depth Historiography and Pragmatic Reading
>
> From Rabbinic Judaism: *peshat* and *derash*
>
> From Christian Theology: *Sensus Literalis* and Spiritual Sense[86]

82. One aspect of SR that I do not discuss in this book is Ochs's "1,000 Cities" project—which certainly depicts Ochs's pragmatist side (see Ochs, *RWV*, 150–204).

83. Ochs, *RWV*, 25.

84. Ochs, *RWV*, 25.

85. Ochs, *RWV*, 27.

86. Here, I follow Gary Slater's keen observation: "It is not difficult to see in Ochs's distinction between plain-sense historiography and pragmatic historiography a replay of his [Ochs's] understandings of *peshat* and *derash*, and the sense in which one's explicit inquiries presuppose implicit guiding principles as central to the methodology of Scriptural Reasoning more generally" (Slater, *C. S. Peirce and the*

According to Ochs, SR allows for readers to engage with passages from the Scriptures on all of these levels. Usually, an SR session begins by highlighting what the specific tradition says is the plain sense of the passage being studied together—participants can decide to take that sense as authoritative, as a guide, or as an initial interpretation. Within a session of SR, readers move about between what seems to be "the meaning of the text in its . . . literary context" and possible deeper or surprising meanings of the passage.[87] In fact, after the traditional plain sense is offered by one of the participants, the next question that often arises within an SR session is: *Does someone want to start by saying what surprises them about this passage?*

In SR sessions, the word 'surprise' functions analogously to how the word 'wonder' operates within ancient and medieval philosophy. "Philosophy begins in wonder" has become a pedagogical cliché, but it remains quite significant when understood in its original sources. First, in Plato's *Theaetetus*:

> SOCRATES: I believe that you follow me, Theaetetus; for I suspect that you have thought of these questions before now.
>
> THEAETETUS: Yes, Socrates, and I am amazed when I think of them; by the gods I am! And I want to know what on earth they mean; and there are times when my head quite swims with the contemplation of them.
>
> SOCRATES: I see, my dear Theaetetus . . . that you were a [true] philosopher, for wonder is the feeling of a philosopher, and philosophy begins in

---

Nested Continua Model, 136). To Slater's summary, I add the terms *Sensus Literalis* and spiritual sense from Christian theology. For Ochs's use of these terms, see Ochs, PSI, 3–53.

87. Ochs, *RWV*, 25.

> wonder. He was not a bad genealogist who said
> that Iris (the messenger of heaven) is the child of
> Thaumas (wonder).[88]

Second, in his *Metaphysics*, Aristotle claims that philosophy begins in wonder because wonder is what makes human beings ask questions; without questions, there would be no philosophy. Third, in his commentary on Aristotle's *Metaphysics*, Thomas Aquinas furthers Aristotle's reasoning on the subject matter: "Because philosophy arises from awe, a philosopher is bound in his way to be a lover of myths and poetry. Poets and philosophers are alike in being big with wonder."[89]

In SR sessions, this kind of wonder gets nurtured by carefully and closely reading small passages from the sacred texts of the Abrahamic traditions. The word SR practitioners tend to use for this is 'surprise': What surprises you from or in this small passage? In philosophical terms, what aspect of this passage leads you to wonder—and would you mind wondering aloud about it for a bit? As Aristotle suggests, what surprises us in a passage might be best stated as a question. As Aquinas defends, what surprises us in a passage might be best stated as a poetic part of the passage—a part of the passage that was neither read nor seen *as poetic* in previous readings of the same passage. Allowing for and encouraging expressions of awe, surprise, and wonder make SR primarily a practice of playfulness—not one of purposefulness.

I claim that Ochs envisions SR as achieving depth and wonder more in the sense we find in Plato's *Theaetetus* than what we gain from Aristotle or Thomas Aquinas. When Ochs says, "Scripture and reader meet each other

88. Plato, *Theaetetus*.

89. Aquinas, *Commentary on Aristotle's Metaphysics*, 66.

at comparable depths,"[90] he means in Plato's terms that a "child of . . . wonder" meets a "messenger from heaven."[91] Within Ochs's understanding of SR, the patterns and words found in the Abrahamic Scriptures represent "messenger[s] from heaven" whereas participants in SR should think of themselves as children of wonder.[92] The significance of the question—does someone want to start by saying what *surprises* them about or in this passage?—cannot and should not be underappreciated or understated for what it means to participate in a SR session. From Ochs's perspective, this question invites the children of wonder (SR participants) to communally and publicly access messages from heaven (the patterns and words of Scripture).

I end on a point made in the introduction: *what makes it hard to write about SR is that no one really knows what will happen after participants address the question of what surprises them.*

90. Ochs, *RWV*, 27.
91. Plato, *Theaetetus*.
92. See Plato, *Theaetetus*.

2

Prudence and Theological Wisdom

Paul Ricoeur *after* David Ford

> I think Paul Ricoeur, along with Karl Barth,
> is among the very greatest Christian minds of
> the twentieth century—two thinkers of the Re-
> formed Protestant tradition who are also deeply
> complementary to each other, and converge,
> one through philosophy [Ricoeur] and the other
> through theology [Barth], on the utter centrality
> of biblical interpretation.[1]

Introduction

David Ford could not be any clearer about his admiration for and reliance on the work of the French
philosopher Paul Ricoeur. Yet, to my knowledge, there is
not a thorough explanation or exploration of the role of
Ricoeur's philosophy in Ford's theology.[2] In this chapter,

1. Ford, ST, 61.

2. Ricoeur is cited but not really engaged in the collection hon-
oring David Ford's theological career; see Greggs et al., *Vocation of
Theology Today.*

I fill that void within scholarship on Ford's theology—as well as in relationship to Ford's reflections on the practice of Scriptural Reasoning.[3]

Paul Ricoeur (1913–2005) spent the majority of his life in France. Born in Dröme, Ricoeur taught at the University of Strasbourgh, the University of Paris, the Catholic University of Louvain, and the University of Chicago. For five years, he also served as an administrator at the University of Nanterre—a suburb of Paris. Ricoeur is one of the few philosophers who takes biblical hermeneutics as a philosophical subject matter—a case I have spent my own philosophical career making,[4] and Ricoeur certainly serves as a model for me in this regard.[5] The books that seem to impact Ford's thinking the most by Ricoeur are the following: *Essays in Biblical Interpretation*, *Figuring the Sacred*, *Oneself as Another*, *The Symbolism of Evil*, and *Thinking Biblically* (co-authored with André LaCocque).[6]

Born in 1948, David Ford is an Irish philosophical theologian—now retired from teaching. Before his retirement, he served as the Regius Professor of Divinity at the University of Cambridge—perhaps the most prestigious faculty position for a Christian theologian in the world. Before Cambridge, he taught at the University of Birmingham. When reading Ford's work, one is often struck by

3. The void concerns the role of Ricoeur's philosophy in Ford's theology and his reflections on SR; there certainly is not a void concerning the relationship between Ricoeur's philosophy and the practice of SR (see Moyaert, "Ricoeur, Interreligious Literacy, and Scriptural Reasoning," 3–26; I engage with Moyaert's wonderful essay in the third section of this chapter).

4. See Goodson, *American Philosophers Read Scripture*.

5. See Ricoeur, *Essays in Biblical Interpretation*; also see Ricoeur and LaCocque, *Thinking Biblically*.

6. Ford has a wonderful essay on Ricoeur's thinking in the collection entitled *Jesus and Philosophy*; see Ford, "Paul Ricoeur," 169–93.

how unapologetic he is about celebrating and engaging the work of authors and scholars he calls "friend": Peter Ochs, Michael O'Siadhail (Irish poet), and Jean Vanier (founder of L'Arche) are only three examples of Ford's friendships. Along with Ochs and Daniel Hardy, Ford is considered one of the founders of the practice of SR. As it happens, Ford is also the son-in-law of Hardy—whose reflections on SR are the subject matter of the next chapter.

Out of the three founders of SR, Ford seems to have written the most about SR—at least, directly about what SR looks like. For this chapter, however, I engage with only one of Ford's defenses and descriptions of SR—a piece Ford published in two different places: "An Interfaith Wisdom: Scriptural Reasoning between Jews, Christians, and Muslims" can be found in both *The Promise of Scriptural Reasoning* (ch. 1) and *Christian Wisdom: Desiring God and Learning in Love* (ch. 8). Throughout this chapter, I cite the version found in Ford's *Christian Wisdom* (*CW*).

In this chapter, I attempt a straightforward explanation of the role of Paul Ricoeur's philosophy in David Ford's thinking—particularly how Ricoeur's philosophy impacts Ford's description and defense of the practice of SR.[7] My claim in this chapter is that Ford sees in SR (a) a social practice that cultivates a certain type of prudence in individual participants and (b) a shared understanding

7. In doing this, I am following Ford's own advice concerning how to further develop SR. Ford explicitly states that Scriptural Reasoning needs Ricoeur for its further development: "One of the marks of Scriptural Reasoning to date has been the variety of its philosophical mentors. . . . I would suggest that, among Christian thinkers, Paul Ricoeur holds great promise. He is a wide-ranging philosopher who has engaged deeply with the Bible, fiction, history, and poetry as well with hermeneutical theory, he has learnt from and critiqued premodern, modern, and postmodern thinkers, he takes seriously both historical and critical study of the Bible and questions about its meaning for today." Ford, "Developing Scriptural Reasoning Further," 217.

of theological wisdom. The connection with Ricoeur's philosophy concerns what types of wisdom the practice of SR cultivates, and I come up with three types: questioning wisdom, argumentative wisdom, and humbling wisdom. After working through the connections between Ricoeur's philosophy and SR, I conclude this chapter by returning to the question of playfulness vs. purposefulness—specifically within Ford's reflections on SR.

"Myth Narrates, Wisdom Argues"[8]

In *Figuring the Sacred*, Paul Ricoeur develops a particular and peculiar version of wisdom—one that brings together, we might say, Athens and Jerusalem. First, Ricoeur defends what I call *questioning wisdom*. According to Ricoeur, wisdom requires "radical questioning": "wisdom passes from the proverb to radical questioning."[9] In other words, biblical wisdom—"the proverb"—requires Socratic behavior.[10] This means that biblical wisdom does not accept the beliefs, norms, and standards of one's given culture or tradition; biblical wisdom in fact mandates a constant and wise questioning of those beliefs, norms, and standards.[11]

Second, Ricoeur introduces what I call *argumentative wisdom*. He contrasts wisdom with mythology:

8. Ricoeur, *Figuring the Sacred*, 252.

9. Ricoeur, *Figuring the Sacred*, 177.

10. See Ricoeur, *Figuring the Sacred*, 177.

11. Ricoeur also argues that biblical wisdom is universal in scope: "Wisdom addresses itself to the human condition in its universal project." Ricoeur, *Figuring the Sacred*, 177. This move to universalism neither abolishes nor eliminates particularity, and I am able to explain the dynamic between particularity and universality better in chapters 3 (Coleridge) and 7 (Hegel).

Can myth fully answer the expectations of acting and suffering human beings? Only partially, inasmuch as it does respond to a form of questioning ... inherent in the very form of lamentation. How long? Why? To this interrogation, however, myth brings only the consolation of order, by situating the supplicant's complaint within a more encompassing framework. But it leaves unanswered one important part of the question, which is not just Why? but Why me? Here the lament turns into an actual complaint ...

With this insight, myth has to change registers. It must not only narrate the origins, in order to explain how the original human condition reached its present state; it also has to explain why such is the case for each and every one of us. This shift leads us from myth to the stage of wisdom. *Myth narrates, wisdom argues.*[12]

Ricoeur's argument concerning the distinction between arguing and narrating provides ground to distinguish between the theological project known as Radical Orthodoxy and the practice of Scriptural Reasoning. The main proponent of Radical Orthodoxy, John Milbank, was a colleague of Peter Ochs's for a time at the University of Virginia. In his magnum opus, *Theology and Social Theory: Beyond Secular Reason*, Milbank argues that the task of Christian theology does not involve out-arguing but rather *out-narrating* other traditions.[13] If one were to take a Radical Orthodox approach to SR, then SR would become a practice where Jewish participants attempt to out-narrate Christian and Muslim participants; Christian participants attempt to

12. Ricoeur, *Figuring the Sacred*, 251–52. Emphasis added.

13. See Milbank, *Theology and Social Theory*, 267–69; although not in reference *Figuring the Sacred*, Milbank actually makes his case against Ricoeur's theory of interpretation.

out-narrate Jewish and Muslim participants; and Muslim participants attempt to out-narrate Jewish and Christian participants. SR does not do this! Instead, SR encourages and nurtures *arguments* between participants. David Ford's distinct contribution to reflections on SR involves the claim that *SR nurtures arguments between participants for the sake of cultivating wisdom*. SR is a unique practice on the terms of Ricoeur's account of wisdom, and without referencing SR Ricoeur states clearly what happens in SR sessions: participants argue over what biblical wisdom looks like based upon short passages from the traditionally sacred texts of Jews, Christians, and Muslims.[14]

Third, Ricoeur defends what I call a *humbling wisdom*.[15] For Ricoeur, wisdom means embodying and performing Jesus's words "whoever loses their life for my sake will find it" (Matt 16:25) in one's "everyday existence."[16] Ricoeur asks, "Have I gone too far in my interpretation of the meaning of wisdom by having it say that 'whoever would save their life will lose it'?"[17] To which he answers, to no one's surprise, that he has not gone "far enough": "For the farther we go down the road of . . . wisdom, the more we are struck by Jesus' invitation . . . to lose one's life 'for

14. In his book *Habermas and Theology*, Nicholas Adams challenges the dichotomy between argument and narrative. Within SR, Adams argues, participants *argue* about biblical *narratives*. While I think Adams is right about that formulation for understanding SR, I still think SR prioritizes arguing over narrating in the way that Milbank means by traditions out-narrating one another. See Adams, *HT*, ch. 10.

15. At one point in *Figuring the Sacred*, Ricoeur critiques thinking of wisdom in terms of humility: "wisdom is . . . tempted to an excess of humility." Ricoeur, *Figuring the Sacred*, 178. In his reflections on Matt 16:25, however, I find that he makes a strong case for a version of wisdom that comes with humility.

16. See Ricoeur, *Figuring the Sacred*, 284–88.

17. Ricoeur, *Figuring the Sacred*, 286.

the sake of Jesus.'"[18] Ricoeur makes it quite clear what this means for intellectuals and scholars who wish to cultivate wisdom in their own lives. According to Ricoeur, this wisdom does not require being Christian or following Jesus in the ways defended and developed throughout the Christian tradition. Rather, "for the sake of Jesus"

> means not to overevaluate my [own] knowledge, caught up as it is in questions of proof and guarantees. . . . For all God's power, God only gives . . . the sign of divine weakness, which is the sign of God's love. To [be wise is to] allow myself to be helped by the weakness of this love.[19]

Ricoeur offers what he calls "a nonchristological, wisdom-oriented reading" of Matthew 16:25, so that the type of wisdom established in the logic of this verse can be extended universally[20] and the type of wisdom established in the logic of this verse entails allowing one's self "to be helped by the weakness of this love" in one's "everyday existence."[21]

SR as a Practice that Cultivates Prudence and Wisdom

Ricoeur's account of wisdom in *Figuring the Sacred* provides enough material for seeing the ways in which Ricoeur's thinking is taken up by David Ford in his reflections on the practice of SR. There are numerous places where Ford engages with Ricoeur's philosophy, all of which are helpful and interesting. However, what I wish to do in this section is to match Ford's reflections on SR and wisdom with Ricoeur's account of wisdom from the previous section. In

18. Ricoeur, *Figuring the Sacred*, 286.

19. Ricoeur, *Figuring the Sacred*, 288.

20. Ricoeur, *Figuring the Sacred*, 284.

21. See Ricoeur, *Figuring the Sacred*, 284–88.

this section, I arrange Ford's reflections on SR in relation to the three points about wisdom in the previous section.

Questioning Wisdom—Like Ricoeur, Ford also finds Socrates to be an exemplar of wisdom. Connecting the practice of SR with the early writing style of Plato, Ford comments:

> Plato['s] . . . early works were fully dialogical, trying to catch the dynamics of Socrates in conversation. . . . For Plato, philosophy was learned and developed through face to face conversation in the context of a whole way of life. . . . In the centuries that followed, the living heart of his philosophical tradition was the conversational teaching of the Academy in Athens.[22]

What does the dialogical style of Plato have to do with the practice of SR? "With regard to Scriptural Reasoning," Ford argues, the "*unreproducible density and dynamics of conversation in small groups gathered around scriptural texts may be central to its practice and to the quality of its collegial scriptural wisdom.*"[23]

What does Socratic questioning have to do with the practice of SR? Ford emphasizes how each religious tradition allows their inherited wisdom to be questioned within the practice of SR: "*The condition for wise Abrahamic practicality is that each tradition allows itself to have its own wisdom questioned and transformed in engagement with the others. This means recognizing them as analogous wisdoms with the potential of worthwhile interplay.*"[24] SR allows participants to challenge the interpretations and

22. Ford, *CW*, 298.
23. Ford, *CW*, 298.
24. Ford, *CW*, 299.

inherited wisdom brought to the study sessions by individual participants.

Argumentative Wisdom—In the previous section, I quickly applied Ricoeur's distinction between argumentative and narrative to the practice of SR. Ford's reflections on SR allow me to further the application. Because of the role of hospitality within the practice of SR, argumentation works better than out-narration. According to Ford, in SR there

> is three-way mutual hospitality: each is host to the others and guest to the others as each welcomes the other two to their "home" scripture and its traditions of interpretations. As in any form of hospitality, joint study is helped by observing certain customs and guidelines that have been developed through experience over time. These are the *prudential wisdom* of the practice of Scriptural Reasoning.[25]

Ford's use of "prudential wisdom" correlates with Ricoeur's category of argumentative wisdom.[26] To extend Ford's metaphor, a good host would not try to out-narrate their guests; a good host, however, welcomes argumentation and correction. Indeed, since ancient Greek philosophy, to be wise and to love wisdom involve maintaining such an openness to argumentation and correction.[27]

The question becomes, what kind of argumentative wisdom does the practice of SR nurture? I do not find a positive answer to this question in Ford's writings, but he helpfully provides what unwise argumentation looks like

25. Ford, *CW*, 279. Emphasis added.

26. See Ford, *CW*, 279.

27. For my own account of prudence, particularly as it relates to Jewish philosophy, see Goodson, "Prudence in the 21st Century?," ch. 2.

within SR: "Christian participants in Scriptural Reasoning have not found it helpful to concentrate on arriving at
doctrinal agreement with Jews and Muslims on the Trinity, christology, and eschatology."[28] Ford calls seeking out
such arguments "an unwise path."[29] Why unwise? Because
it leads "deep into the marshes created by centuries of mis-
understanding and polemics."[30] I concur with this warning
offered by Ford about SR.

Humbling Wisdom—Ford's final point about what I
call argumentative wisdom requires an intense amount of
humility. Humility arises within Ford's reflections on SR
as an intellectual and theological virtue, and both relate to
Ricoeur's development of humbling wisdom.

According to Ford, SR "seeks to be wise"—which
means that it cultivates a certain type of intellectual expectation.[31] Ford claims, "It [SR] does not seek to be normative knowledge or to be the only valid interpretation or to
be demonstrable and invulnerable; rather, it seeks to be
wise."[32] For Ford, SR is a social practice that cultivates a
certain type of prudence in individual participants: this
type of prudence relates to humbling wisdom.

Furthermore, if we match Ford's words with Ricoeur's
promise

> not to overevaluate my [own] knowledge, caught
> up as it is in questions of proof and guarantees.
> . . . For all God's power, God only gives . . . the
> sign of divine weakness, which is the sign of

---

28. Ford, *CW*, 300.

29. Ford, *CW*, 300.

30. Ford, *CW*, 300.

31. See Ford, *CW*, 296.

32. Ford, *CW*, 296.

> God's love. To [be wise is to] allow myself to be
> helped by the weakness of this love . . .[33]

we also come to the conclusion that SR nurtures a shared understanding of theological wisdom. In the case of SR, theological wisdom relates to Ricoeur's humbling wisdom: wisdom involves learning "to be helped by the weakness of [God's] love."[34]

Unsurprisingly, Ford has his own take on humbling wisdom as a theological virtue. About SR, Ford writes,

> [A]ttention to the scriptures helps ensure that emergent wisdom is related to God and God's purposes in history and for the future. Within Scriptural Reasoning perhaps nothing has been theologically more fundamental than the threefold sense that study and interpretation are happening in the presence of God and for the sake of God, in the midst of the contingencies and complexities of a purposeful history, and in openness to God's future and for the sake of God's purposes.[35]

Recognizing God's presence during an SR session is not intended as a claim of theological triumphalism in favor of one tradition's understanding of God. *Recognizing God's presence during an SR session, rather, means practicing SR with a humbling wisdom.* For Ford, this humbling wisdom drives the argumentation, rationality, and reasoning of the practice of SR.

---

33. Ricoeur, *Figuring the Sacred*, 288.
34. Ricoeur, *Figuring the Sacred*, 288.
35. Ford, *CW*, 300.

Ricoeur and SR: Making the Connections Clear and Explicit

Marianne Moyaert makes the connections between Ricoeur's philosophy and the practice of SR quite clear and explicit, and in this section I spell out her argument in order to further substantiate the role of Ricoeur's philosophy within SR. Moyaert's argument builds to this conclusion:

> [T]he practice of Scriptural Reasoning is an excellent embodiment of what Ricoeur had in mind: a practice in which people who belong to different faith traditions become guests in each others' scriptures and learn to read both their own texts and those of others with fresh eyes.[36]

Moyaert gives readers three key premises for arriving at this conclusion—that SR is the kind of practice envisioned by Ricoeur.

First, SR corrects or repairs what Ricoeur identified as the problem of *xenophobia*. In Moyaert's words:

> Ricoeur rejects any kind of particularistic tribalism, according to which believers, belonging to different traditions and speaking different religious languages, somehow inhabit entirely different worlds and so are unable to converse with one another in any meaningful way. The claim that religions are *untranslatable* is, to his mind, an expression of *xenophobia*—fear of the stranger, inspired by the illusory longing of purity. . . .
>
> To be more precise, Ricoeur argues that to overcome xenophobic tendencies that reinforce the contrast between identity and alterity, people are called to become (always imperfect) translators. To translate is to mediate between

36. Moyaert, RSR, 24.

> a plurality of languages, cultures, and religions
> and to preserve the unity of humankind in the
> midst of diversity.[37]

Although I tend to avoid using the word 'tribalism' because of its vagueness, this premise from Moyaert also serves as one of the primary points of this book: SR not only deems *xenophobia* problematic but also embodies and performs correctives to *xenophobia*. In chapters 6 and 7, I argue that these correctives can be called *philia* and *xenophilia* respectively. Moyaert's premise, however, states that treating religious traditions as untranslatable to one another is "an expression of *xenophobia*";[38] the translation of religious traditions to other religious traditions, through the interpretation of scriptural passages, drives SR as a practice. In this way, SR embodies a correction to the expression of *xenophobia*—a correction Ricoeur recommends.

Second, SR keeps religious traditions active and alive in ways that Ricoeur thought were needed. According to Moyaert,

> Traditions, Ricoeur argues, can only stay alive if
> they constantly create themselves anew. As soon
> as traditions are no longer recreated and re-
> newed, they die. From this perspective, it would
> seem that only those traditions capable of wel-
> coming difference in some practice of linguistic
> hospitality will be able survive and maintain
> their identity.[39]

This is a point that cannot be overstated about the practice of SR. There is a legitimate case to be made that the survival of religious traditions within the modern world requires

37. Moyaert, RSR, 12.
38. Moyaert, RSR, 12.
39. Moyaert, RSR, 13.

much more engagement between those traditions. In the modern world, religious traditions have a tendency to close themselves off to other ways of thinking—other systems or traditions. According to Ricoeur, such enclosement will prove their downfall and their ending. From a Ricoeurian perspective, we need practices that put religious traditions in conversation with one another. SR is such a practice.

Third, like Ford, Moyaert emphasizes the metaphor of hospitality for thinking about SR. She comments, "In quite a Ricoeurian way, Scriptural Reasoning presents itself as a praxis of mutual hospitality in which each is both host and guest in relation to the others."[40] This metaphor connects with SR as a practice of argumentative wisdom.

SR embodies Ricoeur's philosophy in terms of correcting *xenophobia*, offering a practice that sustains religious traditions through inter-religious engagements, and providing a way to perform argumentative wisdom through the "praxis of mutual hospitality."[41] For these reasons, Moyaert correctly concludes that SR ought to be understood as an embodiment and performance of Ricoeur's hermeneutical philosophy. Like Charles Sanders Peirce is the *American* philosopher that stands behind the practice of SR, I conclude that Paul Ricoeur is the *French* philosopher that stands behind the practice of SR.

SR as a "Leisure Activity"

On the question of playfulness, I align myself with Moyaert's conclusion that SR works best as a pedagogical practice that has no prescribed end. In her words: "There is no 'fixed rule' that determines the course of [SR] meetings, just as there

40. Moyaert, RSR, 16–17.
41. Moyaert, RSR, 16–17.

is no 'prescribed outcome.'"[42] This means that the practice of SR strictly concerns playfulness.[43] In this chapter, I have focused on David Ford's reflections on the practice of SR. Where does Ford land on the tension between playfulness and purposefulness?

What I described as humbling wisdom earlier in this chapter leads Ford, perhaps somewhat surprisingly, to prioritize playfulness over purposefulness within the practice of SR. His phrase for this, however, is neither musement nor playfulness. Rather, he defends and describes SR as a "leisure activity"![44] What does he mean by this, and how does it connect to humbling wisdom?

David Ford focuses his attention on how to understand SR as a particular kind of *academic* practice. As an academic practice, SR is best understood as a "leisure activity."[45] Ford reasons about it this way:

> Premise 1: "Scriptural Reasoning does not encourage anyone to become an 'expert' in Scriptural Reasoning, as if it were possible to know all three scriptures and their traditions of interpretation in a specialist mode."[46]

> Premise 2: "The usual pattern is for participants to be especially proficient in their own tradition and to be able to 'host' discussion of their scripture, [b]ut at least one of the other traditions is generally outside one's academic specialty . . . so study of that, together with

42. Moyaert, RSR, 17.

43. In relation to the epigraph from Plato's *Republic*: Moyaert defends SR on the terms of Glaucon's first class of goods—a practice can be good "for [its] own sakes, independently of [its] consequences."

44. See Ford, *CW*, 292.

45. See Ford, *CW*, 292.

46. Ford, *CW*, 292.

study of all three together, is more like a leisure or amateur activity. . . ."[47]

Conclusion: Within the academy, SR is best understood as a "leisure activity" that comes with no prescribed scholarly outcomes or results.[48]

In short, SR is a practice that participants do for the sake of the practice. Better put, SR is an academic practice that scholars enjoy and do so only for the sake of the practice.

Ford also makes a theological case for SR as a playful practice. Ford's theological case for SR follows from the argument concerning humbling wisdom earlier in this chapter.[49] In the theological case, SR is not done for the sake of the practice but for the sake of God:

> [S]criptural reasoning's deepest and most comprehensive rationale in all three traditions is that it is done for God's sake. It can be instrumental . . . , but before God it [SR] is above all an end in itself, worth doing because it celebrates the name of God in the company of others who are doing something comparable. As such . . . , it exemplifies the wisdom of God.[50]

SR "exemplifies the wisdom of God" because it has no other end or goal except "for God's sake."[51] This represents Ford's theological description of SR.[52]

47. Ford, *CW*, 292.

48. See Ford, *CW*, 292.

49. I mean this quite literally: In *Christian Wisdom*, what I describe as humbling wisdom is found on page 300—which leads to Ford's discussion as doing SR for "God's sake" on page 302.

50. Ford, *CW*, 302.

51. Ford, *CW*, 302.

52. In relation to the epigraph from Plato's *Republic*: Ford defends SR on the terms of Glaucon's first class of goods—a practice can be good for goodness sake or for God's sake, "independently of [its] consequences."

In relation to the tension raised in this book concerning playfulness vs. purposefulness, Ford lifts up the playful side of that tension. What he adds to the discussion is the phrase "leisure activity": as an academic practice, SR is a "leisure activity."[53] In my mind, this represents Ford's version of Peircean musement.

53. See Ford, *CW*, 292.

Part 2

The *Reasoning* Aspect of Scriptural Reasoning

What does the word reasoning mean in the phrase Scriptural Reasoning? I have attempted two previous answers to this question,[1] and in Part 2 of this book, I offer two more. In chapter 3, I focus on Daniel Hardy's—another founder of the practice of SR—use of Samuel Taylor Coleridge's Romanticism for thinking through the reasoning of Scriptural Reasoning. In chapter 4, I demonstrate how Muhammad Iqbal's reconstruction of religious reason provides a helpful answer to the question: What is the reasoning of Scriptural Reasoning?

---

1. See Goodson, "Repressing Novelty?"; and Goodson, "Richard Rorty and Scriptural Reasoning."

3 ————————————————————————

Reason and Romanticism

Samuel Taylor Coleridge *after* Daniel Hardy

The point of this chapter concerns how Samuel Taylor Coleridge's Romanticism inspires Daniel Hardy's reflections on reason—and, in particular, the *reasoning* of Scriptural Reasoning. As I did in chapters 1 and 2, I give a bit of biography about both Coleridge and Hardy before the arguments.

Samuel Taylor Coleridge (1772–1834) has been described as a literary critic, philosopher, poet, and theologian. He is partly responsible for Romanticism as a literary and political movement in England in the nineteenth century. While he published numerous books of philosophy and poetry, the work that is most important for Daniel Hardy's appreciation of Coleridge is entitled *Opus Maximum*—written in the 1820s.[1] What matters the most for Hardy's interests and purposes are Coleridge's ideas about

1. Coleridge's *Opus Maximum* serves as the reference point for all of my claims about Coleridge's Romanticism in this chapter; see Coleridge, *Opus Maximum*.

(a) the reality of *Logos* and *Spirit*, (b) the relationship between particularity and universality, (c) resolving the tension between individuality and relationality, (d) re-thinking the faculty of reason after modern philosophy, and (e) the Romantic quest for "primal truth."[2]

Daniel Hardy (1930–2007) was an Anglican theologian and one of the founders of the practice of Scriptural Reasoning. Hardy taught theology at General Theological Seminary, University of Birmingham, and Durham University. The practice of Scriptural Reasoning started in the early part of the 1990s while Hardy served as director of the Princeton Center for Theological Inquiry in New Jersey. Hardy and Ochs developed a deep friendship, and Hardy was Ford's father-in-law (David Ford is married to Deborah, the daughter of Dan Hardy). I met Hardy in Fall 2006 when he spent some time staying with the Ochs's in Charlottesville, Virginia—a year prior to his death. His presence somehow was both gentle and powerful.

In this chapter, I articulate the ways in which Samuel Taylor Coleridge's Romanticism impacts the practice of Scriptural Reasoning through the reflective writings of Dan Hardy. I attend to three essays written by Hardy: "Reason, Wisdom, and the Interpretation of Scripture" (2004), "The Promise of Scriptural Reasoning" (2006), and "Harmony and Mutual Implication in the *Opus Maximum*" (2006). In terms of the tensions worked through in chapters 1 and 2, in this chapter I argue that Hardy favors purposefulness and theological seriousness over playfulness and musement.

So the way the tension arises in this chapter involves a Romanticist emphasis on imagination yet downplaying the role of playfulness within the practice of SR—which comes out in a few different ways in Hardy's thinking. First, Hardy does not buy into the dichotomy usually found within

2. See Hardy, RWIS, 83–88.

Romanticism: making the imagination a higher faculty than reason. Following Romanticism, Hardy accepts the critique of how modern philosophy limits reason too severely; departing from Romanticism, or rather how Hardy repairs the interpretations of Coleridge's Romanticism, what scholars of Romanticism call the faculty of the imagination Hardy defends as a higher reason—limited neither to deduction nor induction. This move allows Hardy to shift from imagination and playfulness to higher reason and theological seriousness. Second, for Hardy, SR becomes the *practice* needed in the late twentieth and early twenty-first century for achieving this higher reason and theological seriousness. While Hardy affirms the conservative or traditionalist aspects of religious communities, religious believers do not achieve higher reason and real theological seriousness by remaining enclosed in their own traditions. SR provides a practice where religious believers conserve and defend their religious beliefs and commitments but also offers (a) a *discipline* that religious traditions alone cannot practice and (b) a *rationality* that neither academic disciplines nor religious traditions can reach. Third, SR's definite ends concerns finding a "primal truth"—which, for Hardy, involves both a relationship with and an understanding of God not achievable without the practice of SR.[3]

This chapter proceeds as follows. First, I briefly clarify what I mean by Romanticism. Second, I discuss Hardy's interpretation of Coleridge's Romanticism and how it inspires his view of SR. Third, I say a bit more about Hardy's understanding of the practice of SR—particularly the priority of purposefulness and theological seriousness over playfulness.

3. See Hardy, RWIS, 83–88.

What Is Romanticism?

I begin with Michael Ferber's definition of Romanticism, along with his description of how Coleridge fits within the philosophical tradition of Romanticism. Ferber highlights three aspects in regards to Coleridge's Romanticism: (a) the priority of the imagination over reason, (b) the prominence of benevolence, and (c) the role of Enlightenment philosophy within Romanticism. Ferber's explanations of Coleridge's Romanticism aids in better understanding and recognizing the significance of Hardy's interpretation of Coleridge.

With many caveats, Ferber offers his own definition of Romanticism. He defines Romanticism as

> a . . . set of kindred movements, which found in a symbolic and internalized romance plot a vehicle for exploring one's self and its relationship to others and to nature, which privileged the imagination as a faculty higher and more inclusive than reason, which sought solace in or reconciliation with the natural world . . . , and which rebelled against the established canons of neoclassical aesthetics and against both aristocratic and bourgeois social and political norms in favor of values more individual, inward, and emotional.[4]

Of note are Ferber's claims concerning the privileging of "the imagination as a faculty higher and more inclusive than reason" and rebelling against established "norms in favor of values more individual, inward, and emotional."[5]

Ferber elaborates on the relationship between reason and the imagination in Coleridge's Romanticism. He claims,

4. Ferber, *Romanticism*, 10.
5. Ferber, *Romanticism*, 10.

> Most Romantics believed that the imagination was the supreme human faculty, superior to reason or understanding, and when it was fully exercised humans achieved a godlike vision and creative power. For Coleridge . . . , the imagination is a mediating and unifying power of the mind: it unites the other faculties and united the mind itself with nature. It is creative . . . and "poetic" . . . [T]he imagination produces something new, by a deeper kind of diffusion and refusion through symbols.[6]

Ferber maintains that a key feature of Coleridge's Romanticism involves the priority of the imagination over the faculty of reason, and once this priority is in place then we can appreciate the ways in which the imagination mediates and unifies the powers of the mind. Through the imagination, therefore, new meanings and symbols are produced and realized.

Coleridge's Romanticism continues and embodies Immanuel Kant's Enlightenment philosophy, according to Ferber. He argues that Coleridge aligned himself with Kant's Enlightenment philosophy,[7] and we find this mostly in how Coleridge turned from societal norms to Kant's motto: "Use your own understanding!"[8] Like Kant's recommendation in "What Is Enlightenment" to think for oneself in medicine, politics, and religion,[9] Coleridge "seemed to renounce politics in favour of . . . a rich interior life."[10] At the very least,

6. Ferber, *Romanticism*, 54.

7. "The old view of Romanticism as a reaction against Enlightenment rationalism in the name of emotion or the intuitions of the heart . . . is misleadingly simplistic." Ferber, *Romanticism*, 30.

8. Kant, "What Is Enlightenment?," 133.

9. See Kant, "What Is Enlightenment?," 133–41.

10. Ferber, *Romanticism*, 96.

Coleridge challenged and renounced the philosophical, political, and religious norms of his day.

Lastly, according to Ferber, benevolence is a crucial aspect of Coleridge's Romanticism. He says, "Coleridge . . . sought effective benevolence through renovation of government, religion, and education."[11] The moral aspect of Coleridge's Romanticism involves his emphasis concerning benevolence—an emphasis that encourages individuals to change norms, not for the sake of changing norms, but for the sake of the good.

How Coleridge Inspires Hardy's View of SR

In this section, I outline Hardy's interpretation of Coleridge's Romanticism in seven points. However, the movement of this section is not a straightforward outline. The movement of this section involves thinking and writing in two different directions: (a) comparing and contrasting Hardy's interpretation of Coleridge with Ferber's interpretation of Coleridge and (b) demonstrating the ways in which Hardy's interpretation of Coleridge inspires his understanding of the practice of SR.

Hardy begins by making explicit Coleridge's theological reasoning in his Romanticism. Hardy claims that Coleridge sought "to *discover the order of all things in relation to their source in God, and thus to recover what it is for them to be formed in their fullness by reference to the purposes of God.*"[12] This first point becomes foundational for understanding the remainder of Hardy's interpretation of Coleridge's Romanticism and how it inspires his understanding of the practice of SR.

11. Ferber, *Romanticism*, 31.
12. Hardy, HMI, 35.

Second, Hardy implements and unpacks the phrase "mutual implication"—which serves as a key phrase within his interpretation of Coleridge's Romanticism.[13] According to Hardy, "He [Coleridge] sought . . . to find the *mutual implication* of all things—and the methods by which they were to be understood—with the finding of truth and goodness in God."[14] The phrase, "mutual implication,"[15] leads Hardy to reflect upon the relationship between particularity and universality in Coleridge's Romanticism. Hardy says that the "issue for Coleridge was how realities *are constituted* and, while remaining fully themselves, are also *mutually implicated*, that is fully related to each other both proximately and also ultimately by reference to God."[16] In other words, Coleridge's Romanticism affirms the particularity of individuals while also strives to achieve universality through "mutual implication"—through concrete relationships.[17]

On Hardy's understanding, this relationship between particularity and universality is part and parcel of the practice of SR. SR affirms the particularity of religious believers and their identity in relation to their religious traditions. Through studying sacred texts together, SR also strives to achieve universality through "mutual implication"— through the concrete relationships fostered and nurtured by the practice.[18] At one point, for instance, Hardy describes SR in these terms:

> [T]he strength of SR [is] that its participants can bring strong views to the table. But reading

13. See Hardy, HMI, 36.
14. Hardy, HMI, 36.
15. Hardy, HMI, 36.
16. Hardy, HMI, 38.
17. See Hardy, HMI, 38.
18. See Hardy, HMI, 36–38.

and reasoning our Scriptures together is what "holds" these diverse views in a "space" where we take responsibility not only for our own views, but also for others'. Our mutual hospitality is a *responsible* one, which itself anticipates peace between the Abrahamic traditions and also begins to make a contribution to repairing a world filled with oppression and suffering. "*Above all*" . . . is the ongoing practice of reading and reasoning our Scriptures together, in which we learn . . . the possibilities of complex harmony between us. There is indefinitely more still to learn from our Scriptures, our readings and our reasonings.[19]

Within the practice of SR, individuals take responsibility for their own identity and views. Furthermore, Hardy thinks that individuals take responsibility for the views of others. This responsibility for the views of others exercises what Hardy calls the "mutual hospitality" found within the practice of SR.[20] Mutual hospitality must be understood on the terms of mutual implication.

Notice in the above quotation that Hardy describes SR as a certain type of "space"—one that brings together and encourages "diverse views" from participants who "bring strong views to the table."[21] He intends this as a strong criticism of the spaces cultivated, established, and nurtured in the academy—an intention he makes quite explicit in another essay. In "Reason, Wisdom, and the Interpretation of Scripture," he claims, "In response to the secular academics, we should . . . build a new community of reasoning practices, a community of those who are held and sustained by

19. Hardy, PSR, 207.
20. See Hardy, PSR, 207.
21. Hardy, PSR, 207.

the task of fathoming the density of meaning of Scripture."[22]
Toward this end,

> Christian-Jewish-Muslim "Scriptural Reason-
> ing" provides a way forward [in relation to
> leaving behind the spaces provided in the acad-
> emy]. On the one hand, what this seeks to do is
> identify clearly what is at stake in diverse forms
> of biblical interpretation. The differences lie not
> only in diverse forms of reasoning but also in
> their social counterparts, oppression and ex-
> clusion. What is found is that these follow "the
> dyadic logic of oppression and exclusion" . . . in
> which contrasting practices of interpretation are
> irresolvable, and are used to divide and oppress
> people. Those engaged in . . . Scriptural Reason-
> ing seek to find a transcendent possibility of
> "repairing" this difference-that-is-oppression.[23]

Hardy sees SR as repairing the type of intellectual spaces
cultivated, established, and nurtured within the academy.
Echoing Coleridge's Romanticism, this is the way that
Hardy uses SR to challenge and renounce philosophical,
political, and religious norms of the late twentieth and early
twenty-first century.[24] If Ferber is correct in connecting

22. Hardy, RWIS, 79–80.

23. Hardy, RWIS, 81.

24. In terms of challenging religious norms, Hardy claims, "SR
challenges what is frequently the everyday view of religions in the
West, that they are primarily general systems of beliefs, ideas, and
practices that can be 'held' alongside each other in some overarching
frame of reference, for example as instances of a category called 'religion' or 'religions' within a secular public sphere, thereby enabling
them to be treated 'equally' (as a 'plurality') or encouraging them
to engage with each other ('pluralism'). Instead, SR concerns itself
with the primary discourse of God in the particularities of the Abrahamic traditions, as seen through their particular interpretation of
their particular Scriptures, not in order to compare them and derive

this aspect of Coleridge's Romanticism with Kant's Enlightenment philosophy, then we should also conclude that Hardy promotes this aspect of Enlightenment philosophy as well—challenging and renouncing inherited norms that come with problematic logics.[25]

Before continuing with Hardy's account of SR, I need to take a step back and acknowledge the various stances concerning the relationship between Enlightenment philosophy and the practice of Scriptural Reasoning. The question concerning this relationship has been one of the most fruitful debates within the Society of Scriptural Reasoning. In *Scripture, Reason, and the Contemporary Islam-West Encounter*, for instance, we are given at least four views concerning this relationship: (a) SR affirms Enlightenment philosophy; (b) SR both affirms and critiques Enlightenment philosophy; (c) SR critiques Enlightenment philosophy; and (d) SR affirms Enlightenment philosophy for its Christian and Jewish participants, but SR's ultimate purpose is to provide healing between Enlightenment philosophy and Islam. Martin Kavka's chapter in *Scripture, Reason, and the Contemporary Islam-West Encounter* represents the first position: according to Kavka, SR becomes "senseless" if not understood as the affirmation and continuation of Immanuel Kant's and G. W. F. Hegel's

---

what is thought to be common to them, but in order to allow them to disagree or agree and by doing so illuminate the others." Hardy, PSR, 186.

25. In the conclusion, I defend a different aspect of Kant's philosophy that relates to SR. Instead of his Enlightenment thinking, I defend Kant's deontology because I believe that SR is a practice that lifts up the dignity of its participants. Although I do not make this move in the conclusion, following Hardy I could assert that the academy deeply struggles with lifting up the dignity of human persons—which means that the practice of SR repairs that problem as well.

Enlightenment philosophies.[26] Kavka claims that the next two views concerning the relationship between Enlightenment philosophy and the practice of Scriptural Reasoning find representation in Steven Kepnes's and Basit Koshul's chapters also in *Scripture, Reason, and the Contemporary Islam-West Encounter*: "for Koshul, Scriptural Reasoning both exemplifies and critiques Enlightenment thinking, while for Kepnes, Scriptural Reasoning only critiques it [Enlightenment thinking]."[27] While these three views—Kavka's, Kepnes's, Koshul's—do not lend themselves to an obvious take on the tension between playfulness and purposefulness within SR, Yamine Mermer's view on the relationship between Enlightenment philosophy and the practice of Scriptural Reasoning involves an explicit defense of SR as a purposeful practice. She writes,

> The purpose [of SR] is to heal modernity. More specifically, Scriptural Reasoning is an attempt to repair specific kinds of suffering that are not being attended to by the academic community. Within this context of Scriptural Reasoning, an

26. Kavka writes that the key aspect of SR concerns the feature of "foreigners ask[ing] questions that 'natives' have forgotten should be questions at all"—which leads Kavka to a Hegelian description of SR: "In Hegel, and in Scriptural Reasoning, both Self and Other exist as Self *and* Other as a member of both 'us' *and* 'them.' There is difference *and* a recognized likeness. Only in this way, by attending to what happens in the conversational dynamics of Scriptural Reasoning, [we come] to see that it is not simply opposed to [Enlightenment] philosophy but also at one with [Enlightenment] philosophy." Kavka, "Is Scriptural Reasoning Senseless?," 137, 141.

27. Kavka, "Is Scriptural Reasoning Senseless?," 135. See Kepnes, "Islam as Our Other, Islam as Ourselves," 107–22; see Koshul, "Qur'anic Self, the Biblical Other," 9–38. Kavka claims that Koshul could retitle his essay as "Enlightenment as Our Other, Enlightenment as Ourself." See Kavka, "Is Scriptural Reasoning Senseless?," 135.

> interesting question is how the Qur'anic scrip-
> ture can contribute to the resolution of that
> suffering. This question is especially important
> given the widespread assumption that Islam
> and the West are basically incompatible: Islam
> did not develop in a secular environment and
> hence it has not been tamed to fit the terms of
> modernity. Scriptural Reasoning, however,
> does not view this situation as a challenge but
> as an opportunity. It sees in Islam the potential
> to infuse religion with a new life and thus to
> contribute with valuable resources of healing
> . . . in the modern world. If Islam has "failed"
> to adapt itself to the demands of the Enlighten-
> ment . . . , it has to be said that this "failure"
> may prove to be not so detrimental in the end;
> for a lack of adaptation to the Enlightenment
> project, may translate into a bonus, putting
> Islam in a rather advantageous position in the
> debate with modernity.[28]

One the one hand, according to Mermer, Christian and
Jewish participants of SR cannot help but practice SR as
part of the Enlightenment project. On the other hand:
Muslim participants contribute to SR as a prophetic voice
critiquing the Enlightenment project, *and* Muslim participants benefit from SR because it provides a practice that
helps heal the division between Islam and modernity. For
Mermer, SR's relationship with Enlightenment philosophy
turns the purpose of SR into one of the healing problems
caused by modernity.

Given what has been explained thus far, Hardy's position on this matter seems to be closest to Koshul's: SR
both affirms and critiques Enlightenment philosophy. My
own stance is closest to Kavka's: SR affirms and continues

28. Mermer, "Islam," 69–70.

the Enlightenment philosophies of Kant and Hegel. However, I remain challenged by and take very seriously the
positions represented by Kepnes, Koshul, and Mermer
(Mermer's stance shows up again in Table 1, located at the
end of the next chapter)—which means that I strongly disagree with Kavka's claim that SR becomes "senseless" if not
understood as the affirmation and continuation of Kant's
and Hegel's Enlightenment philosophies.[29]

Returning to Hardy's account of SR: third, Hardy
distinguishes between extensity and intensity within
Coleridge's Romanticism. According to Hardy,

> [D]ealing with the full scope of existing things—
> their "*extensity*"—in all their actual differen-
> tiation and complexity happens only with full
> attention to the *intensity* of God's identity in
> God's creation of, and love for, the world. Ironi-
> cally, we can *know* the world in all its complexity
> (extensity) only insofar as we are most attentive
> to the God that God is (intensity), because the
> one is made actual by the other, and we can *live*
> satisfactorily in the one only insofar as we are
> attentive to the love that God is.[30]

SR provides a disciplined practice of "intensity," in Hardy's
sense of the word from this passage, which leads to an "extensity" in terms of coming to know "the full scope of existing
things."[31] He elaborates about what he means by extensity:
"One way of describing Coleridge's endeavor is to say that it
embraced the span of everything—its full extensity—while
seeking the relatedness of all things according to the character of each."[32] Within SR, "the character of each" participant

29. See Kavka, "Is Scriptural Reasoning Senseless?," 133–48.

30. Hardy, HMI, 39-40.

31. Hardy, HMI, 39.

32. Hardy, HMI, 43.

remains intact—in terms of their religious beliefs, commitments, identity—while in pursuit of the Romantic journey
toward "full extensity": what it looks like, what it means, to
"embrace . . . the span of everything."[33]

Fourth, Hardy defends "an ongoing teleological
dynamic" on the terms of Coleridge's Romanticism.[34] He
comments, "Coleridge's concern was with the entire *span*
of knowledge and reality as . . . prospectively available, seen
both formally and in concrete actuality, and its *integration
for the human mind in an ongoing teleological dynamic*."[35]
Hardy thinks of SR as a discipline, exercise, and practice
that integrates human minds "in an ongoing teleological
dynamic."[36] For instance, he claims:

> [T]he determination to bring about . . . a finding
> of primary discourse of God in the engagement
> *between* the Abrahamic traditions' interpreta-
> tions of their Scriptures, without attempting to
> stand outside of them or to generalize from what
> is found in them, constitutes the very simple *rai-
> son d'etre* of Scriptural Reasoning.[37]

The "teleological dynamic" pursued within SR concerns
"finding [a] primary discourse of God."[38] For Coleridge,
the *Logos* serves as the teleological goal—*Logos*, in the
Christian use of the word, simply is the one-word des-
ignation for a "primary discourse [about] God" (John
1).[39] SR brings human minds together—traditioned by

---

33. Hardy, HMI, 43.
34. See Hardy, HMI, 43.
35. Hardy, HMI, 43.
36. Hardy, HMI, 43.
37. Hardy, PSR, 186.
38. Hardy, HMI, 43; Hardy, PSR, 186.
39. Hardy, PSR, 186.

Christianity, Judaism, or Islam—and what drives their minds, teleologically, involves "finding [a] primary discourse about God."[40] Hardy identifies this simply as the reasoning of Scriptural Reasoning: "the very simple *raison d'etre* of Scriptural Reasoning."[41]

Next, Hardy emphasizes the Romanticist desire for coherence. Hardy explains how individuality and relationality lead to the concept of coherence in Coleridge's Romanticism:

> [T]here is no point when each in its individuality is not also related to others, or their relationship is not conditioned by their particularities. . . . [T]his is . . . to "summarize" their relatedness, [Coleridge seeks] to *move toward notions of their coherence*, and to start on the way to what might be their *ultimate coherence*, a coherence that would be found in their origins and fulfilment.[42]

When Hardy talks about the "density of meaning" found within sacred texts, he means by that phrase what Coleridge means by "coherence."[43]

For Hardy, SR provides a practice that achieves this Romanticist notion of coherence. For instance, Hardy says this about the "density of meaning": "What is it we should be seeking in the Scriptures? The answer . . . is that we should—and can—agree to seek the density of meaning found there that implicates both God and us."[44] How does he apply this to SR? He writes, "[T]he variety of ways of Scriptural Reasoning . . . , through the ongoing mutual correction of many

40. Hardy, PSR, 186.
41. Hardy, PSR, 186.
42. Hardy, HMI, 43–44.
43. Hardy, HMI, 44.
44. Hardy, RWIS, 75.

of us working together, arrive[s] at a fuller approximation to the depth of scope of the meaning of Scripture."[45] Hardy's emphasis on "the ongoing mutual correction" serves as the way that individuality and relationality lead SR participants to an "ultimate coherence": "a coherence . . . found in their origins" (the Scriptures) "and fulfillment" (the teleology discussed in the previous point).

Sixth, Hardy introduces the logic of abduction in Coleridge's Romanticism. According to Hardy, "*Reason* [is] where the observer form[s] explanations, in what is called *abduction*, and achieved fuller description by means of ideas."[46] Six pages later, he writes,

> The *movement of attraction* is identified by Coleridge by using a term known . . . as "abduction." Logically this is often seen as the postulating of a possible explanation, a "third" form of reasoning beyond—but resourcing—induction and deduction . . . [I]n Coleridge . . . , we find that abduction is "*the being drawn toward the true center*" of all, the Logos and the Spirit.[47]

As both Hardy and Ochs point out, abduction connects Peirce's pragmatism with Coleridge's Romanticism. In my judgment, however, Hardy has it correct here when he says that abduction "is often seen as the postulation of a possible explanation" yet Coleridge does not use it in this way.[48] So Coleridge and Peirce might use the same word, but what they mean by it differs.[49]

45. Hardy, RWIS, 88.

46. Hardy, HMI, 45.

47. Hardy, HMI, 51.

48. See Hardy, HMI, 51.

49. About his use of abduction, Peirce says, "Abduction is the process of forming explanatory hypotheses. It is the only logical operation which introduces any new idea." Peirce, "Nature of Meaning,"

In my own understanding of Coleridge's Romanticism, abduction names the work of the *Spirit* (the third person of the Trinity) that draws believers and thinkers toward the *Logos* (the second person of the Trinity). Hardy emphasizes that this is not the work of the imagination, on the terms of Coleridge's Romanticism, but simply a different function of the faculty of reason than what other modern philosophers allow reason to do. I move on to the seventh point because it concerns what this different function of reason looks like.

As a point of contrast between Ferber's and Hardy's interpretations of Coleridge's Romanticism: Hardy claims that Coleridge *never* shifts from reason to the imagination but makes a case for different levels of reason. In Hardy's words,

> So the Spirit . . . raises . . . the human intellect
> [to] the capacity of Reason, and in the will the
> capacity for love [benevolence], the two together
> making it possible to think—and enact—things
> in their fullest relations. Without that, human
> apprehension remains cognitively and volition-
> ally at lesser levels, and will be incapable of
> the higher levels of reason and love needed for
> higher spheres.[50]

Hardy thinks that other interpreters of Coleridge's Romanticism miss the way in which Coleridge never leaves behind the faculty of reason. Rather, Coleridge orders and ranks the faculty of reason based upon how we are able to think fully and truly about nature, other persons, and ultimately God. Hardy capitalizes "Reason" to signify the highest order of reason, which is the part of the faculty of reason used by

---

216. This is precisely the meaning of abduction of which Hardy attempts to differentiate Coleridge's use.

50. Hardy, HMI, 46–47.

the Spirit to draw human beings to the Logos.[51] In Hardy's words: "In . . . 'being drawn [toward the true center]', human beings are most truly enabled to affirm themselves and the order of all things, as they are illuminated in Reason."[52]

On Hardy's terms: *the name Scriptural Reasoning signifies that the type of reason achieved within the practice of SR ought to be understood as the highest form of the faculty of reason.*[53] This is what I mean by labeling Hardy's reflections on the practice of SR as Romanticist.

This seventh point also includes the role of benevolence in Coleridge's Romanticism. Ferber's interpretation of benevolence in Coleridge's Romanticism comes across as if benevolence is directed only toward other human persons. Hardy disagrees with this interpretation of benevolence—what Hardy calls "love" in the above passage—in Coleridge's Romanticism.[54] For Hardy, benevolence ought to be directed primarily toward God. Hardy thinks that SR practitioners participate in SR to show benevolence toward God. SR has definite ends for Hardy, and these definite ends are theological through and through. The benevolence that comes out within the practice of SR becomes a possibility only because it represents the excess of the benevolence directed toward God by and through SR participants. SR participants demonstrate benevolence toward God by treating all of the texts in front of them as sacred. Treating the texts

51. See Hardy, HMI, 46–47.

52. Hardy, HMI, 52.

53. "Always as attentive as they can be to each other's Scriptures, those who engage with each other in SR *always* do so as 'reasoners'." Hardy, PSR, 186. Emphasis added. Note the differences and similarities between Hardy's sentence with my claim in chapter 1 that while not all scriptural reasoners are trained as philosophers, all scriptural reasoners participate in this Peircean-inspired philosophical community that bases itself on how God is graphed through Scripture.

54. See Hardy, HMI, 46–47.

as sacred might be given several descriptions—all of which, according to Hardy,[55] serve as fine descriptions of SR—but what it means theologically concerns uncovering together "the elemental discourse of God."[56]

Playfulness, Purposefulness, and Theological Seriousness in the Practice of SR

To the extent that higher reason and imaginative thinking might be taken as synonymous within Coleridge's Romanticism, I simply wish to think through a possible tension in Hardy's reflections on SR. On the one hand: usually, imaginative thinking and playfulness go hand-in-hand within the history of philosophy—especially modern philosophy.

55. Hardy offers this set of descriptions about SR: "Some would express this in terms of a 'practical unity of reason' already found in Scriptural Reasoning, or a 'wisdom' found through learning the 'languages of wisdom,' or the 'peace' that is found in the intensely social process of inter-traditional readings, as *persons* are *related* through *texts*. These . . . are different ways of expressing what happens through the gathering of people—with their different embodiments of wisdom, of reasoning, as different persons—in peace. It is more than such words usually convey: it recovers the Reason of the Scriptures themselves." Hardy, PSR, 202.

56. Hardy prefers this description of SR: "[T]he different traditions of interpretation, both in and between the Abrahamic traditions, *enlarge* reasoning. . . . The capacity of Scriptural Reasoners patiently to engage with these enlargements, and with the insights which they nourish in each other, is a matter of great importance; indeed, the 'listening' necessary to this probably needs to become more explicit in the agenda of SR. This may be the way in which, out of its expansions, reasonings may be *re-gathered* and *referred back* to the Reason implicit in the Scriptures themselves . . . to the 'elemental discourse of God.' In other words, the re-gatherings and redirection of reasonings may be [what] uncovers the Reason of Scripture." Hardy, PSR, 202.

My claim in this sentence might be too broad, but I am thinking of Immanuel Kant's wonderful paragraph in the *Critique of Judgment* that captures this point:

> The cognitive powers brought into play by this representation are here engaged in a free play, since no determinate concept restricts them to a particular rule of cognition. Hence the state of the mind in this representation must be one of a feeling of the free play of the powers of representation in a given representation for a cognition in general. Now a representation . . . involves . . . imagination for bringing together the manifold of intuition. . . . This state of free play of the cognitive faculties attending a representation by which an object is given must admit of universal communication: because cognition . . . is the one and only representation which is valid for everyone.[57]

On the other hand, perhaps there is no tension in Hardy's reflections on SR? Perhaps Hardy's shift from the faculty of imagination to higher reason in his interpretation of Coleridge's Romanticism provides implicit ground for him to bluntly prioritize purposefulness and theological seriousness over playfulness within the practice of SR.

I say bluntly because he comes out strongly against SR being a practice of playfulness in relation to offering a variety of interpretations of Scripture. This is what Hardy says against such playfulness: in SR, "a good deal more is at stake" than "the 'free play' of differing interpretations."[58] He goes on to identify this "more" with "the possibility of truth itself."[59] Hardy concludes that this should be considered

57. Kant, *Critique of Judgment*, 48–49.
58. Hardy, RWIS, 82.
59. Hardy, RWIS, 82.

"primal truth."[60] This identification of "primal truth" as what is at stake in the practice of SR represents Hardy's priority of theological seriousness over playfulness.[61] SR's definite ends, therefore, concerns finding a "primal truth."[62]

This "primal truth" involves theological knowledge.[63] For Hardy, it involves both a relationship with and an understanding of God not achievable without the practice of SR. Relationally, SR participants experience more of the fullness of God's *presence* because of the multiplication of Abraham's children *present* together around their sacred texts. Conceptually, SR participants come to know more about who God is through the theological engagements nurtured by the discipline of SR—studying narratives about God's character. As a practice, SR must become and remain theologically serious in order to achieve these theological ends.

On the contrary, I say that SR must be understood *primarily* as a practice of playfulness in relation to how it allows for a variety of interpretations of small passages from the sacred texts of the three Abrahamic religious traditions. With much admiration for Hardy's life and thinking, I contend that SR is a practice of Peircean musement—not a practice that takes part in a Romantic quest for "primal truth."[64] Peircean musement entails the following:

> There is a certain agreeable occupation of mind which, from its having no distinctive name, I infer is not as commonly practised as it deserves to be [and] indulged in moderately. . . . Because it involves no purpose save that of casting aside all serious purpose . . . , it is Pure Play. Now,

60. See Hardy, RWIS, 83–88.
61. See Hardy, RWIS, 83–88.
62. See Hardy, RWIS, 83–88.
63. See Hardy, RWIS, 83–88.
64. See Hardy, RWIS, 83–88.

> Play, we all know, is a lively exercise of one's powers [of imagination] . . . It bloweth where it listeth. It has no purpose, unless recreation. The particular occupation I mean . . . may take either the form of [a]esthetic contemplation . . . or that of considering some wonder in . . . the Universe . . . , or some connection between [the] two . . . , with speculation concerning its cause. It is this last kind—I will call it "Musement" on the whole—that I particularly recommend. . . . One who sits down with the purpose of becoming convinced of the truth of religion is plainly not inquiring in scientific singleness of heart . . . and must always suspect himself of reasoning unfairly. So . . . let religious meditation be allowed to grow up spontaneously out of Pure Play without any breach of continuity, and the Muser will retain the perfect candour proper to Musement.[65]

For anyone unfamiliar with Peirce's philosophy, this passage represents his clearest and deepest description of musement; it can be found in the eighth paragraph of Peirce's essay, "A Neglected Argument for the Reality of God."

Is SR primarily a practice of musement and playfulness or purposefulness and theological seriousness? Contrary to Hardy's Romanticist description of the practice of SR, which prioritizes purposefulness and theological seriousness over playfulness, I conclude this chapter by making the following claims about SR as a practice of musement and playfulness. What does it mean to consider SR primarily as a practice of musement and playfulness?

---

65. Peirce, "Neglected Argument for the Reality of God," 435.

(a) SR provides a way to practice "Pure Play"— "as it deserves to be" practiced and to do so in moderation.[66]

(b) At its best, SR "involves no purpose save that of casting aside all serious[ness]" for a definite amount of time and in an intellectually safe space.[67]

(c) SR requires "a lively exercise of one's powers" and should be understood as a time and place to exercise those powers for the sake of intellectual "recreation."[68]

(d) For some, SR might be best thought of as a practice of "aesthetic contemplation"; for others (as it is on the terms of Ochs's use of Peirce's semiotics), SR might be best thought of as the consideration of "wonder in . . . the Universe"; at its best, SR certainly offers ways to combine these two.[69]

(e) SR should not claim to serve as a practice where its participants become "convinced of the truth of [their own] religion"; if SR violates this rule, then it should lead to suspicion concerning "reasoning unfairly."[70] The positive side of this rule involves allowing and seeing SR as a practice based upon "free play" or "pure play."[71]

(f) In my experience, SR consistently serves as a practice where a type of "religious meditation"

---

66. See Peirce, "Neglected Argument for the Reality of God," 435.
67. See Peirce, "Neglected Argument for the Reality of God," 435.
68. See Peirce, "Neglected Argument for the Reality of God," 435.
69. See Peirce, "Neglected Argument for the Reality of God," 435.
70. See Peirce, "Neglected Argument for the Reality of God," 435.
71. See Peirce, "Neglected Argument for the Reality of God," 435.

occurs "spontaneously out of Pure Play";[72] the variety of interpretations—most of which I could never have arrived at or thought of one of my own—conjured up during a SR session lead to combinations of conviction, illumination, and novelty that no other practice makes possible for me.

These claims represent what I mean by calling and defending SR as a practice of Peircean musement—a practice that allows for playfulness without having to determine ahead of time, or even during the practice, any definite ends or goals.

72. See Peirce, "Neglected Argument for the Reality of God," 435.

4

Reconstructing Religious Reasoning

SR *after* Muhammad Iqbal

> We must reread Iqbal. For a time we could imag-
> ine him forgotten, consigned to the oubliettes
> with the other figures of Islamic "modernism"
> from the beginning of this [twentieth] century.
> But he had to come back . . .
>
> In this atmosphere of suspicion and anger
> it is a joy to hear the voice of Iqbal, both pas-
> sionate and serene. It is the voice of a soul that is
> deeply anchored in the Quranic Revelation, and
> precisely for that reason, open to all the other
> voices, seeking in the path of his own fidelity.[1]

Introduction

Why does the Canadian Roman Catholic philosopher
Charles Taylor think that we must reread and return
to the work of Muhammad Iqbal (1877–1938)? Because
Iqbal "speaks to us today," eighty years after his death.[2] In

1. Taylor, "Preface," xi, xii.
2. The phrasing comes from Koshul, "Contemporary Relevance

97

this chapter, I attempt to listen to "the voice of Iqbal" for better understanding the practice of Scriptural Reasoning: a "voice" that Taylor judges as passionate, serene, and shaped by the logic of the Qur'an.[3]

Muhammad Iqbal was a philosopher, poet, and statesperson. He contributed to the development and establishment of Pakistan as a nation-state—considered, by some, as the intellectual founder of Pakistan.[4] Out of all of the thinkers discussed in this book, Iqbal lived perhaps the fullest life of any of these modern philosophers. He was born in British India, educated in Britain and Germany, and worked as an Advocate within the Lahore court system. In addition to publishing several volumes of poetry, Iqbal re-described Islamic philosophy in relation to the wisdom and work of several modern philosophers: Henri Bergson, Immanuel Kant, G. W. F. Hegel, William James, and Friedrich Nietzsche (this is only to name the philosophers I remember Iqbal engaging with). Iqbal's *Reconstruction of Religious Thought* ought to be judged as one of the most important books in the philosophy of religion written in the twentieth century.

In this chapter, I borrow three terms from Iqbal's *Reconstruction of Religious Thought in Islam* and apply those terms to the practice of SR: faith, thought, and discovery. He uses them to reconstruct religious reasoning, and I use them to describe what takes place in a SR study session—to think through the *reasoning process* of SR. My thesis for this chapter is that these three terms capture the three "parts"

---

of Muhammad Iqbal," 56. Koshul also begins his essay with reflections on Taylor's comment that we "must reread Iqbal." Later in this chapter, I engage with Koshul's argument found in "Contemporary Relevance of Muhammad Iqbal."

3. See Taylor, "Preface," xi–xii.

4. See Anjum, *Iqbal*, chaps. 17–27.

of the reasoning process of SR: scriptural (faith), reasoning (thought), and the relational dynamics of the practice (discovery). I conclude the chapter by returning to the tension between playfulness and purposefulness.[5]

The Significance of Reconstructing/Reconstruction

I had not considered the significance of Iqbal's use of the verb "reconstructing" until reading Souleymane Bachir Diagne's (an Iqbal scholar and former student of Charles Taylor's) analysis of Iqbal's *Reconstruction of Religious Thought in Islam*.[6] Before getting into the core of this chapter, I briefly talk about the significance of this verb.

According to Diagne, the significance of "reconstructing" involves how it leads to what he calls Iqbal's "effort to produce independent reasoning."[7] Diagne claims, "The concept of 'reconstruction' is not to be understood as imitation and mechanical adaptation but as the resumption [note: not assumption] of a living movement, leading out of the petrification that happened in the thirteenth century."[8] Diagne continues by arguing that reconstructing, for Iqbal, means "to struggle with oneself"—to make an "effort to produce independent reasoning."[9]

I find this phrase, an "effort to produce independent reasoning,"[10] a potent yet underappreciated way to describe the practice of SR. As a practice, SR allows and encourages its

---

5. I am grateful to Nauman Faizi for reading this chapter and making suggestions on how to improve the argument.

6. See Diagne, "Achieving Humanity," 33–55.

7. Diagne, "Achieving Humanity," 45.

8. Diagne, "Achieving Humanity," 45.

9. Diagne, "Achieving Humanity," 45.

10. Diagne, "Achieving Humanity," 45.

participants "to produce independent reasoning[s]"[11] concerning the interpretation of their own traditionally sacred texts and sacred texts from other traditions—independent, in the sense of different from or even free from, the interpretations that come to be common within religious traditions. I am trying to get at a similar point made by Mike Higton and Rachel Muers about how SR works "with and beyond the plain sense": "[SR] is not a session that consists simply in the group being told what Muslims have made of this text [or passage]."[12] They continue, "The exploration is a matter of the group playing together with and beyond the plain sense of the text—where the plain sense is the most obvious sense it has for the [participants]."[13] Religious believers need space—a time and place—to conjure up different, novel, and unusual interpretations of scriptural passages; religious believers need to be able to *reconstruct* the potential meaning of small scriptural passages without being beholden to the plain sense and the traditional interpretations of those passages. In other words, religious believers need "to produce independent reasoning[s]"[14] in relation to how they interpret small parts/passages of Scripture. SR provides such a practice, such a space, and ways "to produce [such] independent reasoning[s]."[15]

SR *after* Iqbal's Reconstruction of Religious Reasoning

Iqbal addresses the question, "Is Religion Possible?" in a chapter bearing that title in *The Reconstruction of Religious*

11. Diagne, "Achieving Humanity," 45.

12. Higton and Muers, *TP*, 110.

13. Higton and Muers, *TP*, 110.

14. Diagne, "Achieving Humanity," 45.

15. Diagne, "Achieving Humanity," 45.

Thought in Islam. In Iqbal's chapter, I find a precursor to what the process of SR—the process within the practice—looks like. Iqbal's terms for this process are faith, thought, and discovery. Each of these represent a different level of religious reasoning—hence Iqbal's reconstruction of religious reasoning.

Iqbal divides "religious life . . . into three periods": faith, thought, and discovery.[16] About "faith," Iqbal writes, "[R]eligious life appears as a form of discipline which the individual or a whole people must accept as an unconditional command without any rational understanding of the ultimate meaning and purpose of that command."[17] Although Iqbal uses phrases like "obedience" and "perfect submission" for describing "faith," he does not mean them in a conservative way.[18] Indeed, later in "Is Religion Possible?" he says quite explicitly, "Conservatism is as bad in religion as in any other department of human activity" because "[i]t destroys the ego's creative freedom and closes up the paths of fresh spiritual enterprise."[19]

In the process of SR, this sense of faith comes into play because the practice allows and encourages participants to identify with their own religious tradition—we could say their faith tradition. This identification is not supposed to

16. See Iqbal, *RRTI*, 143.

17. Iqbal, *RRTI*, 143.

18. My interpretation of Iqbal's *Reconstruction of Religious Thought in Islam* has benefited a great deal from Sevcan Ozturk's *Becoming a Genuine Muslim*. She describes Iqbal's understanding of "faith" as neither "conservative" nor "progressive" but simply as a first step—perhaps a condition—required to achieve existential genuineness: "In the first period, the human being accepts religious customs without any examination. This category is not concerned with the individual's existential relation to the religious law." Ozturk, *Becoming a Genuine Muslim*, 101.

19. Iqbal, *RRTI*, 145.

highlight one's *authority* in relation to the text being studied and in relation to the other participants. Iqbal provides the reason for this: using one's faith as grounds for authority, within the practice of SR, "destroys . . . creative freedom and closes up the paths of fresh" Scriptural Reasoning.[20]

In relation to the argument I make in chapter 7: while faith remains part and parcel of the practice of SR, it is best not to think of SR as an inter-faith dialogue because doing so comes with two different problems: (a) it leads to a problematic conception of faith—what G. W. F. Hegel considers as faith in terms of truth-as-correctness—and, more in line with the purposes of the present chapter, (b) it restricts the process of SR to this first level of religious reasoning.

Iqbal moves from the level of faith to that of thought: religious reasoning needs to go from "faith" to "thought."[21] "Thought," according to Iqbal, entails "a rational understanding of the discipline and the ultimate source of its authority."[22] Iqbal equates "thought" with "a kind of metaphysics," but it sounds like a soft metaphysics: "a logically consistent view of the world with God as . . . part of that view."[23] In other words, I can use Iqbal's notion of thought to describe the process of SR and still argue that SR ought to be considered a post-metaphysical practice.[24]

20. Here I am playing with Iqbal's wording; see Iqbal, *RRTI*, 145.

21. See Iqbal, *RRTI*, 143.

22. Iqbal, *RRTI*, 143.

23. Iqbal, *RRTI*, 143.

24. Without using the phrase post-metaphysical, Ozturk offers a post-metaphysical interpretation of Iqbal's use of "thought": "In the second category, the individual attempts to establish a rational understanding of the law . . . , and this period . . . requires a rational foundation . . . to be established through . . . objective reflection." Ozturk, *Becoming a Genuine Muslim*, 101. Ozturk claims that what she means by "objective reflection" resembles Søren Kierkegaard's

In SR sessions, the rules of engagement nurture what Iqbal means by thought. The process of SR works best, not when everyone properly identifies their own faith tradition, but when the conversation remains focused on the words in front of everyone without anyone going off script(ure). Iqbal speaks of logical consistency, and within SR logical consistency means working through the logic of Scripture but limiting one's judgments to this logic only to the passage everyone has in front of them. Because of faith, this logical consistency relates to "the ultimate source" as "part of that view": this is what it means, within SR, to treat all of the passages as "Scripture."[25] However, I maintain that the *process* of SR works best if thought remains prioritized over faith: if Scriptural Reasoning keeps a proper order between the adjective and the noun.

In what they call the "ambiguity of voice," Mike Higton and Rachel Muers capture quite well the significance of keeping the adjective and noun in order for the practice of SR.[26] They write,

> [SR] often involves participants speaking in ambiguous voices. A Christian reader might playfully suggest a reading of part of [a] Qur'anic text—and it is in part an offering to the Islamic readers of a way in which *they* could read their text, a gift to the Muslims qua Muslims, from a non-Muslim who cannot but sit lightly on the gift. But sometimes . . . the suggestions made are as much suggestions to the Christians and the Jews: does the reading I am suggesting for this Qur'anic passage not suggest analogous readings of Christian and Jewish texts, or analogous

existentialist use of "objective." Ozturk, *Becoming a Genuine Muslim*, 31–33.

25. See Iqbal, *RRTI*, 143.

26. See Higton and Muers, *TP*, 110–11.

> theological ideas? Might it be an idea Christians
> or Jews can appropriately borrow or adapt, even
> if it turns out not to be a sustainable Islamic
> reading? Might it in fact be *more* [of] a sugges-
> tion for Christian and Jewish participants than
> a suggestion for the Muslims? It is worth asking
> . . . who [someone speaks to rather than who
> they speak for].[27]

When practicing SR, the faith of the participants at the
table should not trump the communal reasoning required
for working through the logic of Scripture exclusively of the
texts in front of the participants.

In the practice of SR, communal reasoning ought to
remain prioritized over individual faith. By communal reasoning, I mean (in the words of Higton and Muers) that SR

> is exegetical, but it is not as such *an* exegesis of
> the text. That is, it does not produce anything
> like a coherent, well-defined construal of the
> text as a whole. . . . Rather, it is a series of playful
> explorations of the text. The pattern . . . is [like]
> exploring a maze, not knowing which openings
> are going to lead to dead ends . . . , which to
> pathways to follow. . . . The conversation finds
> its way—but finding a way and drawing a map
> are not the same.[28]

This metaphor of "finding the way," not "drawing a map,"
captures the reasoning—or what I am calling in this chapter
the "thought"—of Scriptural Reasoning.

Iqbal argues that the shift from "thought" to "discovery" is a shift from metaphysics to psychology.[29] According
to Iqbal, "discovery" occurs when "religious life develops

27. Higton and Muers, *TP*, 111.

28. Higton and Muers, *TP*, 110.

29. See Iqbal, *RRTI*, 143.

the ambition to come into direct contact with . . . Ultimate Reality."[30] This sounds metaphysical, not psychological. So what does Iqbal mean by shifting from the metaphysical to the psychological?[31] He answers this question in this way: "It is here [discovery] that religion becomes a matter of personal assimilation of life and power . . . ; the individual achieves a free personality . . . by discovering the ultimate source of the law within the depths of his own consciousness."[32] Iqbal echoes a Kantian argument that links freedom with following an internal law.[33] "Discovery" names a "higher religion" for Iqbal:

> [A] higher religion, which is only a search for a larger life, is essentially experience and recognized the necessity of experience. . . . It [discovery] is a genuine effort to clarify human consciousness, and is, as such, as critical of its level of experience as Naturalism is [critical] of its own.[34]

For Iqbal, "discovery" names the highest level of religious reasoning.[35] He calls it "psychological" because it makes a religious believer aware of "ultimate reality" in a personal

30. Iqbal, *RRTI*, 143.

31. Ozturk answers this question in a helpful way: "What Iqbal means by displacement of metaphysics by psychology is that, in this period of religiousness, the individual does not need the answers to his metaphysical questions or any intellectual or rational quest anymore. His quest is now to achieve a more intimate relation to God. . . . This relationship between the individual and God helps him discover himself as a unique self." Ozturk, *Becoming a Genuine Muslim*, 123.

32. Iqbal, *RRTI*, 143.

33. His analysis of Kant can be found on pages 144–45.

34. Iqbal, *RRTI*, 143–44.

35. Iqbal, *RRTI*, 143–44. Therefore, what Part 2 of this book establishes is that SR is a practice that cultivates, nurtures, and requires higher reasoning in general (Hardy's Romanticism) and higher religious reasoning in particular.

or relational sense, *and* it means that one becomes self-critical on the basis of one's religious reasoning.[36] "Faith" follows a discipline; "thought" helps one see the world logically and metaphysically; "discovery" joins the discipline of "faith" and the new perceptions of "thought" for the purposes of developing a conscious relationship with God and a healthy form of self-criticism.[37]

In SR sessions, participants often leave commenting on how they now see a passage from their own scriptural text anew. In my experience, seeing one's own Scripture in new lights occurs more often than learning something new about one of the other traditions. Because the rules of engagement require focusing on the texts in front of everyone, interpretations taken for granted become challenged; usually, such challenges do not come with any resolution for participants during the course of a SR session.

Iqbal emphasizes relationality and self-criticism as what "discovery" makes possible,[38] and this emphasis provides a way to begin to grasp the relational dynamics within the practice of SR. These two categories are nurtured deeply during the process of SR. Because of the playfulness of SR, however, there is no way to say ahead of time what the results will be concerning relationality and self-criticism; they both look different for different participants. In classical philosophical terms, I can say *that* these two categories are

36. In Ozturk's words, "In the final period, religious life seeks to establish a closer contact with God, the Ultimate Reality, and the third stage is the ultimate point of religiousness for Iqbal. . . . [T]he individual establishes a subjective relationship with religion by what Iqbal regards as 'personal assimilation.' In other words, the individual exists in religion through his own conscious action of assimilation. . . . [T]he human being becomes the vicegerent of God, the third stage in the development of the self." Ozturk, *Becoming a Genuine Muslim*, 101.

37. See Iqbal, *RRTI*, 143–45.

38. See Iqbal, *RRTI*, 143–45.

nurtured during the reasoning processes of SR; I cannot say *what* these categories look like for individual participants during and after the reasoning processes of SR.[39]

Iqbal and the Need for Inter-religious Engagements

According to one of the leading scholars of Iqbal's work and the first Muslim participant in SR, Basit Bilal Koshul, Iqbal's notion of discovery grants us reason to engage with members from other religious traditions—as well as those in no religious tradition at all. Koshul offers three premises toward the conclusion that Iqbal's notion of discovery, within his reconstruction of religious reasoning, requires religious believers to participate in some form of inter-religious engagements (the third premise brings Peirce's philosophy into the equation):[40]

> Premise 1: "[I]nstead of the 'gaze of others' being a cause of fear, suspicion, and *xenophobia*, it becomes a resource of self-discovery, self-awareness, and self-affirmation."[41]
>
> Premise 2: "Iqbal's voice, echoing the message of the Qur'an, calls upon individual human beings, different communities, and different traditions to build a 'renewed self' that views an affirmation and acceptance of the alien other as a uniquely valuable resource for increased

39. Perhaps this distinction is one of the ways to respond to David Ford's warnings about writing about SR: when writing about SR, one needs to prioritize *that*-ness over *what*-ness in the claims one makes about SR.

40. For a fully developed account of the relationship between Iqbal and Peirce, see Ochs, "Iqbal, Peirce, and Modernity," 79–94.

41. Koshul, "Contemporary Relevance of Muhammad Iqbal," 57.

self-awareness, deepened self-understanding, and genuine self-affirmation."[42]

Premise 3: "Iqbal and Peirce teach us that it is indeed possible 'to seek out and define oneself' using references found in the other's tradition. . . . Iqbal's 'religion of science' is a religion that opens itself up to the findings of science in its quest for sharpened self-understanding and self-awareness. Peirce's 'science of religion' is a science that opens itself up to the wisdom of religion for sharpened self-understanding and self-awareness. This opening up is not done under duress or under conditions imposed from the outside but is the result of an inner calling and a sense of self-confidence. The inner-calling and self-confidence allows the self to view that alien other not as an existential threat but as an existential need for the growth and affirmation of the self."[43]

These premises lead to Koshul's overall conclusion: Iqbal's "contemporary relevance" concerns how his reconstruction of religious reasoning requires religious believers to participate in in-depth forms of inter-religious engagements within the twenty-first century.[44]

Of course, I share in that conclusion. In this book, I am trying to make a case for SR as an in-depth form of inter-religious engagement for and within the twenty-first century. Koshul and I are in agreement about how inter-religious engagements serve to overcome the problem of

42. Koshul, "Contemporary Relevance of Muhammad Iqbal," 57.

43. Koshul, "Contemporary Relevance of Muhammad Iqbal," 85–86; Koshul quotes Taylor in the first sentence (see Taylor, "Preface," xi).

44. See Koshul, "Contemporary Relevance of Muhammad Iqbal," 56–87.

xenophobia, and my claim in this book is that SR repairs the multiple manifestations of *xenophobia* experienced in the twenty-first century. Without applying his argument to the practice of SR,[45] Koshul captures well the relational dynamics of the practice of SR.

I turn my attention to some of the particularities of Koshul's third premise given above. The dynamic, emphasized by Koshul, between religion and science relates to the playful dynamic between Scripture and reason within SR.[46] Within SR: Scripture "opens itself up to the findings of" reason—findings that come from the communal reasoning that takes place during the practice of SR of wrestling with the words everyone has in front of them.[47] Also within SR: reason "opens itself up to the wisdom of" the scriptural passages being studied during a SR session.[48] *The reasoning aspect of Scriptural Reasoning must be fostered by the logic of scriptural passages, and the scriptural aspect of Scriptural Reasoning must be guided by the communal reasoning of the participants*—developed through argumentation, critical engagement, and self-criticism.

45. Koshul has numerous reflections on SR as well. For only three of them, see "Rules of Scriptural Reasoning"; "Scriptural Reasoning and the Philosophy of Social Science"; and "Theology as a Vocation."

46. Seemingly, Koshul has not yet taken a position on the playfulness vs. purposefulness tension within SR; however, I infer that he would emphasize playfulness over purposefulness because of the ways in which he writes on the dynamic relationship between religion and science.

47. See Koshul, "Contemporary Relevance of Muhammad Iqbal," 85.

48. See Koshul, "Contemporary Relevance of Muhammad Iqbal," 85.

Playfulness in Scriptural Reasoning, Seriousness in Religious Reasoning

I agree with Bashit Koshul and Charles Taylor: in the twenty-first century, Iqbal's "voice" needs to be heard! In this chapter, I have listened to Iqbal's "voice" in order to articulate and better understand the practice of SR. SR provides a process for Iqbal's version of religious reasoning to be nurtured, practiced, and transformed from theological seriousness to philosophical playfulness.

Muhammad Iqbal treats faith, thought, and discovery in a purposeful and theologically serious way for developing the religious life and reconstructing religious reasoning. I believe that Iqbal remains right to approach religious life with theological seriousness. Such theological seriousness, however, need not be adopted when applying faith, thought, and discovery to the practice of SR. The conclusion of the previous chapter fits the conclusion of this chapter as well: SR is a practice best understood on the Peircean terms of "free play" or "pure play."[49]

To further clarify SR as a practice of playfulness or purposefulness, I conclude Part 2 with a table concerning the question of musement vs. theological seriousness, playfulness vs. purposefulness, pragmatism vs. semiotics.[50]

49. See Peirce, "Neglected Argument for the Reality of God," 435.

50. The following table represents my own inferences about how to place and understand individual scholars and theorists about SR in relation to the tensions I have raised about SR; it does not represent what each scholar and theorist might say about themself in relation to this tension within SR.

SR Practitioners and Theorists	Musement/ Playfulness/ Semiotics	Pragmatism/Purpose- fulness/Theological Seriousness
Peter Ochs	SR as a semiotic, triadic practice SR as a practice of musement that encourages wonder	SR as the pragma- tist community of enquirers seeking the truth SR as a purpose- ful practice toward Abrahamic peace-making
David Ford	SR as an academic leisure activity; SR is practiced for God's sake	
Daniel Hardy		SR as a theological- ly serious practice, with definite ends
Basit Koshul	SR resembles the playful dynamic between religion and science in modernity	
Nicholas Adams		SR as a purposeful practice with a definite end toward friendship
Mike Higton and Rachel Muers	SR as a playful experiment in reading Scripture	

SR Practitioners and Theorists	Musement/ Playfulness/ Semiotics	Pragmatism/Purpose-fulness/Theological Seriousness
Yamine Mermer		SR as a purposeful practice for healing the problems of modernity, includ-ing the relationship between Islam and the Enlightenment
Marianne Moyaert	SR as a playful inter-religious dialogue	
	SR as a playful pedagogical practice	

My own thinking about SR falls more in line with the side of musement, playfulness, and semiotics; in part 3, however, I develop Nicholas Adams's description of SR as a purposeful practice with a definite end toward friendship.

Part 3

The *Relational* Dynamics of Scriptural Reasoning

ended chapter 4 by reiterating my case for SR as primarily a practice of playfulness. In Part 3, I only consider SR as a practice of purposefulness—the definite end or outcome of SR and the relational dynamics of SR being friendship and *philia*. In chapter 5, I focus on Nicholas Adams's rigorous reflections on the practice of SR—which Adams presents in relation to the work of the German philosopher, Jürgen Habermas. What drives chapter 5 are my two disagreements with Adams: discovering (in Iqbal's sense of the word) is a better verb than "making" (Adams describes SR as a practice where participants "make deep reasonings public"), and the need to distinguish between communicative action and communicative rationality in Habermas's philosophy. In chapter 6, I build from Adams's emphasis on friendship as the definite end or outcome of SR and offer Martha Nussbaum's account of friendship and *philia* to SR practitioners and scholars.

5

From Making to Discovering

Jürgen Habermas *after*
Nicholas Adams

P eter Ochs narrates the practice of Scriptural Reasoning
in relation to the American philosophy of C. S. Peirce
whereas Nicholas Adams seems to think that the theory of
communication—found in German philosopher Jürgen
Habermas's work—offers a more helpful philosophical
foundation for understanding the practice of SR.[1] While I
agree with Adams's turn to Habermas's theory of communication for understanding the practice of SR, in this chapter
I demonstrate how Habermas's theory of communication
becomes helpful only when we distinguish between two of
his (Habermas's) theories: the theory of communicative action and the theory of communicative rationality.

1. Taking stock: Peirce is the American philosopher standing
behind SR; Ricouer is the French philosopher standing behind SR;
Iqbal is the Pakistani philosopher standing behind SR; and Habermas
is the German philosopher standing behind SR.

Habermas's theory of communicative action and his theory of communicative rationality are not inter-change-able phrases: readers can have one without the other, and the theories do not necessarily depend on each other. Communicative action concerns how two or more individuals relate to one another in everyday (non-philosophical) interactions—namely through body language and patterns of speech. Communicative rationality is a philosophical theory that seeks to (a) explain the peacefulness of argumentation involving both agreements and disagreements, and (b) the logical tools involved to repair broken forms of argumentation and engagement. Early in his writing career, Habermas concerned himself with systematic "distortions"; later in his career, however, Habermas takes a decidedly Kantian turn and argues for the rational ability of every individual to use communicative reasoning. This means that even if an individual finds themself in a distorted and problematic system, where there is no *communicative action* occurring, then they can employ their abilities and skills of *communicative rationality* without the need to rely upon the societal system in which they find themself.[2]

My claim in this chapter is that SR provides such a context no matter how broken the Abrahamic traditions are, and the thesis of this chapter is that Adams's call for "making deep reasonings public" within the practice of SR requires communicative rationality—not communicative action. This chapter proceeds as follows. First, I articulate the significance of Nicholas Adams's gift of Habermas's philosophy to SR. Second, I explain Adams's use of the phrase "making deep reasonings public" and shift the verb to how SR allows

2. I encourage readers to first read my chapter on the differences between communicative action and communicative rationality in Habermas's philosophy: see Goodson, "Communicative Reason and Religious Faith in Secular and Post-Secular Contexts."

its participants to *discover their deep reasonings*—discover in the sense developed in the previous chapter. Third, I synthesize Adams's use of the phrase "making deep reasoning public" with Habermas's theory of communicative rationality. I conclude by reflecting on the significance, within SR, of comparing and contrasting Peirce's semiotics with Habermas's theory of communicative rationality.

Adams's Gift of Habermas's Philosophy to Scriptural Reasoning

The Scottish philosophical theologian Nicholas Adams makes a strong case for Jürgen Habermas's theory of communication as the best philosophical interlocutor for understanding how argumentation, conversation, and debate work within the practice of SR. In particular, Adams claims that the practice of SR can be described as the process of "making deep reasonings public." While this phrase does not come from Habermas's writings (I narrate the genealogy of the phrase late in this chapter), Adams rightly thinks that it reflects the role of religious reasoning within Habermas's theory of communicative action. Adams gifts Habermas's philosophy of communication to SR in two different publication: the final chapter of *Habermas and Theology* and "Making Deep Reasonings Public" in the edited volume *The Promise of Scriptural Reasoning*.

Adams concludes his book *Habermas and Theology* with a chapter entitled "Scriptural Reasoning and Scriptural Difference." In the preceding chapter, entitled "Narrative and Argument," Adams goes to great lengths to defend the position that the disciplines of philosophy and religious studies need to account for both "argument" and "narrative." Analytic philosophy and a rigid scientific approach to religious studies tend to emphasize "argument," while Continental philosophy and a post-liberal approach to religious studies tend to focus either on "narrative" as a writing style or the study of narratives within philosophical and religious traditions. Adams finds in Habermas's theory of communication a way to hold together both "argument" and "narrative," but he also makes the judgment that Habermas does not remain loyal to his own best insights on holding these two together.[3] Adams concludes the "Narrative and Argument" chapter with the recognition that if we stick with the concepts of "argument" and "narrative," then "argument" will always be given more weight. He says, "*Only* an attention to actual practice can do justice to the relationship between narrative and argumentation."[4] This insight leads Adams to the practice of Scriptural Reasoning because SR attends to *narratives* yet sustains constant *argument* about those narratives and the positions that arise from those narratives.

One way to read Adams's *Habermas and Theology* is to say that Habermas's theory of communication requires a practice like SR precisely because of this balance between "argument" and "narrative."[5] That seems a correct reading. I add the claim that SR needs Habermas's theory of communication in the sense that Habermas's theory strengthens and sustains reflections upon the practice of SR. Adams offers three claims relating to what I consider his gifting of Habermas's theory of communication to SR.

---

3. Adams writes, "Habermas tries to leave it [narrative] behind by developing a procedural ethics [based on argumentation alone]." Adams, *HT*, 220.

4. Adams, *HT*, 233.

5. Note Adams's own claim: "Scriptural reasoning seems to me a be a better practice for coordinating different traditions in genuine argumentation than his [Habermas's] project of discourse ethics." Adams, *HT*, 252.

First, Habermas's theory of communicative action does not block SR from being understood as a philosophical practice of argumentation. What Habermas's philosophy helps scriptural reasoners recognize is that religious reasoning is both "metaphysical" and "post-metaphysical." SR provides a practice where the metaphysical and the post-metaphysical can be sorted out through a process of argumentation and public debate.

Second, Adams offers a distinction for reflecting on SR found within Habermas's theory of communication. Adams writes,

> [C]onsider . . . Habermas's distinction between "normatively ascribed" and "communicatively achieved" agreement. It [concerns] the difference between (a) claims which appeal to *already accepted* background assumptions, and which invite a "yes" response, and for which . . . a "no" would be intolerable and (b) claims which invite a "yes and no" response and which are genuinely open to contradiction. For Habermas, a communicatively achieved "yes" is hard won, and therefore binds those who agree on it together in some socially significant way.[6]

Adams struggles in articulating how this distinction applies to SR,[7] but the application seems to be: the normative

6. Adams, *HT*, 247.

7. Adams's struggle is noteworthy: "Scriptural reasoning offers . . . [a] bleaker scenario. There is genuine argumentation between participants, and it is by definition across different traditions. Most kinds of 'yes' that arise are certainly hard won in Habermas's sense. But are they 'normativaley ascribed' or 'communicately achieved'? Here Scriptural Reasoning is an anomaly for Habermas. By 'normatively ascribed,' Habermas refers to assumptions *within one tradition* that secure agreement. By 'communicatively achieved,' he means the generation of agreement *across* traditions without appeal to norms held

ascription of SR concerns how scriptural reasoners treat ancient texts as sacred and worthy of study whereas the communicative achievement concerns the arguments over the meaning and sense of the narratives being studied.

Third, neither Habermas's theory of communication nor the practice of Scriptural Reasoning is subject-centered.[8] Each requires the participants to be bound to a greater process of reasoning. In Adams's words: "In Habermas's theory, participants *become bound* by the process of argumentation. In Scriptural Reasoning, they are *already bound* by their own traditions."[9] Adams goes on to explain how the binding to their own religious traditions gets supplemented by being bound by the process of studying texts together "with members of the other two traditions."[10] Against Habermas, Adams prefers to identify this binding—being bound by the process of studying texts together "with members of the other two traditions"—with "the possibility of friendship." For Habermas's theory of communication, processes of

---

to be true in only tradition. But participants in Scriptural Reasoning acknowledge *only* the norms of their own tradition, and subject them to no higher authority except that of God." Adams, *HT*, 247. Adams loads the assumptions against SR here, and he fails his own correct insight—found on the previous page—that what makes SR interesting philosophically is that scriptural reasoners tend not to "use their religious faith as a rhetorical means for blocking requests for reasons." Adams, *HT*, 246.

8. Subject-centered is a phrase often employed by Habermas to articulate the tendency within modern philosophy to give the power of reason to the individual alone, independent of communication and relationality; subject-centered becomes Habermas's shorthand for categorizing the role of rationality and reason in the philosophical theories of Rene Descartes, Baruch Spinoza, John Locke, David Hume, and Immanuel Kant.

9. Adams, *HT*, 248.

10. Adams, *HT*, 249.

reasoning do not lead to friendship but to justice, solidarity, and tolerance.[11]

Three levels of rationality—and its connection with relationality—arise from this analysis: (a) subject-centered rationality, which does not require relationality; (b) relationship-generated rationality bound by a process of reasoning that leads to justice, solidarity, and tolerance (Habermas's position); and (c) relationship-generated rationality bound by a process of reasoning that makes friendship possible (Adams's position). Reflecting on SR in terms of a relationship-generated rationality, where subjects are bound to one another in a process of reasoning, becomes the primary way in which Adams gifts Habermas's philosophy to SR. Adams does not equate SR with Habermas's theory but, rather, demonstrates how SR walks along with Habermas away from subject-centered rationality and then takes a further step from Habermas's theory of communication toward a consideration of the possibility for friendship.[12]

11. For instance, when Giovanna Borradori asks Habermas if the categories of "friendship" and "hospitality" are better, morally, than the notion of "tolerance"—because of the condescending and paternalistic nature of "tolerance"—Habermas never addresses the categories of "friendship" and "hospitality" in his answer. See Habermas, *Divided West*, 74–75.

12. Instead of the threesome of justice, solidarity, and tolerance, Adams shrinks Habermasian expectations down to "consensus": "The most striking thing about the context of Scriptural Reasoning is not consensus but friendship. . . . Consensus can be measured and managed, and to that extent is an appropriate object of a theory like Habermas's. Friendship is altogether more confusing, and even the most sophisticated philosophical accounts of it somehow repeat the absurdity of the hopeless lover who tries to persuade the other to love him by using arguments. . . . Friendships is nonetheless the true ground of Scriptural Reasoning, and who can give a good overview of that?" Adams, *HT*, 243. In the next chapter, I attempt an "overview" of friendship as the "ground of Scriptural Reasoning"; readers can

Making Deep Reasonings Public

Adams credits the Christian theologian, C. C. Pecknold, with originating this phrase.[13] In his substantial and wonderful review of Jeffrey Stout's *Democracy and Tradition*, Pecknold makes the following judgment on Stout's book:

> Stout's real service to religious traditionalists may be to call for a revival in communal Scriptural Reasoning about public life, not as *the* discursive authority, but as a normed and improvisational discourse which "makes public" the deepest reasons internal to the great religions.[14]

There are several main characters in Stout's *Democracy and Tradition*: Ralph Waldo Emerson, John Dewey, Jürgen Habermas, Stanley Hauerwas, Alasdair MacIntyre, John Milbank, John Rawls, and Richard Rorty. In his review of Stout's book, Pecknold never mentions Habermas's role in *Democracy and Tradition*. Adams, however, corrects the neglect of Habermas's relationship to the phrase coined by Pecknold in the sense that this phrase relates as much to Habermas's theory of communication as it does to Stout's "service to religious traditionalists."[15]

The phrase, "making deep reasonings public," concerns a process of argumentation and communication. Adams claims that he

> agree[s] with Habermas: either there really can be argumentation, in which case one should try to give an account . . . of the reasonings that

---

determine if my attempt qualifies as "good."

13. Adams writes, "The sentiment [of making explicit deep reasonings] is Jeffrey Stout's; the phrasing is Chad Pecknold's." Adams, *HT*, 241.

14. Pecknold, "Democracy and the Politics of the Word," 209.

15. See Stout, *Democracy and Tradition*, 1–15.

support it, or there cannot, in which case one must—intolerably—give up on public debate.[16]

Giving an account of reasonings that support particular positions becomes a necessary aspect of argumentation within Habermas's theory of communication, and Adams concurs with Habermas on this point. Without such an account, argumentation cannot occur in public contexts. SR ought to be considered a practice within a public context because it does not remain within the bounds of a singular religious tradition. What type of reasoning occurs with the public context of the practice of SR? Adams answers this question with these words: "The process of 'reasoning' is not just the teasing out of interpretive issues, but also the making explicit of 'deep reasonings.'"[17] According to Adams, two actions occur within SR: teasing out interpretations and "making explicit . . . deep reasonings." Together, these two actions get SR on the way to meeting Habermas's theoretical expectations for what constitutes argumentation.

Adams further explains how SR makes deep reasoning explicit. He distinguishes between "(a) definitions, axioms and presuppositions, (b) logics and rules for reasoning, and (c) actual chains of reasoning."[18] He argues that religious traditions encounter one another—in the public context of SR—"with long histories of (c)s, where communal identities are expressed at a profound level."[19] To meet Habermas's standards of argumentation, Adams claims: "It is not just the exposure of (a)s that need to happen in argumentation; it is the rehearsal of (c)s *as expressions of identity*."[20] SR

16. Adams, *HT*, 238.
17. Adams, *HT*, 241.
18. Adams, *HT*, 242.
19. Adams, *HT*, 242.
20. Adams, *HT*, 242.

allows and nurtures such rehearsal of "expressions of identity." Adams explains: "Scriptural reasoning is a practice of 'publicising' deep reasonings, so that others may learn to understand them and discover why particular assumptions are attractive or problematic. *Scriptural Reasoning makes deep reasonings public*."[21] By applying these distinctions to the practice of SR, SR fulfills Habermas's theoretical expectations for argumentation—for giving "an account . . . of the reasonings that support" the claims that accompany the two actions of teasing out interpretations and "making explicit . . . deep reasonings."

He does not stop here. Adams says that SR takes a further step than Habermas's theory of communication requires in the sense that SR sees "deep reasonings" not as "obstacles to debate, but as conditions for conversation, friendship, and mutual understanding."[22] Adams remains committed to this third level of forging friendship through the practice of SR—which goes beyond Habermas's expectations for and standards of justice, solidarity, and tolerance.

This difference between Adams's expectations of friendships and Habermas's standards of justice, solidarity, and tolerance takes an even sharper turn when Adams introduces the role that vulnerability plays in the practice of SR. Adams writes,

> Depth is not obscurity . . . : the acknowledgement of depth is a recognition that it takes time to plumb. Scriptural reasoning models the discovery that making deep reasoning public is not only risky—because one makes oneself vulnerable when revealing what one loves—but time-consuming.[23]

21. Adams, *HT*, 242.
22. Adams, *HT*, 242.
23. Adams, *HT*, 242.

Adams identifies three characteristics of SR as a practice of argumentation and communication, and these characteristics involves the demands it makes of its participants: it becomes "risky" for its participants; it makes its participants "vulnerable" to one another; and it requires perseverance of its participants because it is a "time-consuming" practice. Although vulnerability is not the focal point of this passage, reflecting on the role of vulnerability helps clarify the ways in which Habermas's and Adams's arguments differ in terms of their expectations relating to argumentation and communication.

Professor of Communication at the London School of Economics Lilie Chouliaraki rightly claims that while "Habermas's work centrally engages with questions of justice and solidarity, he [Habermas] is suspicious of the role that human vulnerability may play as an act of cosmopolitan education in the West."[24] She offers two reasons relating to Habermas's suspicions about vulnerability.[25] She claims,

> Assuming that linguistic interaction is the means by which the public sphere coordinates action-in-the-world, Habermas regards human vulnerability as an obstacle to such coordination, in that it displaces questions of justice and solidarity onto a benevolent but de-politicized

24. Chouliaraki, "Mediating Vulnerability," 106.

25. She actually gives the two reasons twice within her essay: once more simplified and another time more complex. For purposes of this chapter, I quote in the body the more complex set of reasons because it introduces Habermas's theory of communicative action in a more explicit way. The more simplified version reads, "The politics of vulnerability, he argues, limits rather than enhances our 'responsibility to act in the world': on the one hand, it turns questions of inequality into the consumption of state services for the poor and, on the other, it lends itself to media manipulation, replacing the moral force of suffering with television spectacle." Chouliaraki, "Mediating Vulnerability," 107. I return to these words later in this chapter.

welfare state, while its mediation relies on an inauthentic visuality that sensationalizes rather than rationalizes its cause. The public sphere that is presupposed and reproduced in this process remains, consequently, restricted to the nation-states and solidarity is understood as un-mediated dialogue within the nation-state, in-evitably leaving distant others the public scope's of responsibility.[26]

Habermas's concern with expecting vulnerability involves how vulnerability tends to replace justice and solidarity.

So far in this chapter, I have asserted over and over that Adams *adds* another layer to Habermas's theory of communication—one that involves the expectations of friendship and vulnerability. It turns out, however, that this third layer is not only unwelcomed within Habermas's theory of communication but serves as a threat to his own expectations of and standards for justice, solidarity, and tolerance. If this is all there is to say about the matter, then it seems that Adams has described SR in terms that counter Habermas's theory of argumentation and commu-nication. It becomes clear, on Adams's account, that mak-ing deep reasonings both explicit and public—within the practice of SR—requires vulnerability on the part of the participants. Does this requirement of vulnerability shut down the possibility of Habermas's philosophy serving the interests and purposes of SR? I address this question in the next section; before that, however, I raise one criticism of Adams's use of the phrase "making deep reasonings pub-lic" in describing the practice of SR.

Why "making deep reasonings public"? Adams's an-swer seems to be that this phrase captures what occurs with-in a SR session, and making deep reasonings public results

26. Chouliaraki, "Mediating Vulnerablity," 109.

in friendship among the participants of this practice. On the contrary, I say that SR does not allow participants to *make* their "deep reasonings public" but to *discover* their deep reasonings. This returns us to the playful aspect of SR. The phrase "make deep reasonings public" sounds assertive, intuitive, and overly confident in one's own beliefs and ways of reasoning; SR, rather, encourages hypothesis-making, musement, and taking guesses about what texts say and mean— this playfulness aids participants in *discovering* what might become "deep reasonings," but one of the main purposes of the practice of SR concerns how the practice itself repairs the "deep reasonings" that we hold resulting from both subject-centered rationality and traditional interpretations of Scripture. Adams emphasizes how "making deep reasonings public" within the practice of SR leads to the "definite end" of friendship; I wish to focus on the playfulness of the practice of SR where it becomes a practice that gives religious believers space and time to *discover* their deepest reasonings in communicatively rational ways.[27]

Deep Reasonings and the Theory of Communicative Rationality

Simply put, Habermas's theory of communicative action would be the one best applied to the activities within religious traditions and the dynamics at work when members of different religious traditions encounter one another in the routines of their daily lives. Habermas's theory of communicative rationality would be the one best applied to discursive practices of argumentation and communication

27. If the verb "making" is taken as "in the making," then discovering and making might not be as far apart as I suggest here. For the role of "in the making" within modern philosophy, see Miner, *Truth in the Making*.

that are separate from the routines of our daily lives and more academic in nature and purpose.

With this distinction in place, SR clearly fits the latter: the theory of communicative rationality. Since the word "clearly" risks fallacious thinking,[28] for simplicity's sake I quote Adams's own observation:

> Scriptural reasoning is . . . not a focal practice for its participants, but an extension . . . that is not necessarily warranted by the theologies of the participants' traditions, and may—on certain interpretations—even be forbidden by them.[29]

For readers who prioritize simplicity in arguments, then this explanation suffices. They may skip to the first full paragraph on page 137.

To put it much more complexly: the fact that the religious traditions are broken means that intellectuals within religious traditions need an academic outlet for the sake of exercising their own rationality. SR sessions provide such an outlet to their participants. For Habermas, the university setting becomes the primary context where communicative reason gets achieved and modeled. For religious believers both within and without the university, SR sessions offer a public context and setting where making deep reasonings explicit can be achieved, modeled, and shared no matter how broken the religious traditions of which the participants are members.[30]

28. According to the rules of modern logic, words like "clearly" and "obviously" signal the possibility of the proof surrogate fallacy within an argument.

29. Adams, *HT*, 240. Adams continues: "Scriptural reasoning thus means, for its participants, acknowledging that their particular traditions do not encourage their joint reading of scripture, but doing it anyway." Adams, *HT*, 240.

30. In Adams's words, "Scriptural reasoning models a practice of

In his essay, "Making Deep Reasonings Public," Adams claims that participants in SR do not "claim any special theological or textual expertise, and this renders them vulnerable to in an academy for which expertise is the goal of study, and in an educational milieu for which information is the most highly prized commodity."[31] This means that SR is much more like Habermas's theory of communicative rationality because Habermas himself displays distaste for the over-specialization of the modern academy where monologues occur more than dialogues between several disciplines. According to Habermas, one of the goals of academic life concerns the achievement of a coherent and unifying discourse where scholars are freed from their own subjectivities and work toward particular conclusions reached through the process of communicative rationality. In order for this achievement to occur, scholars need to (a) cultivate a "decentered understanding of the world" and (b) participate in the process of a "pragmatic logic of argumentation" where research, teaching, and writing lead to normative judgments which can be shared through the particular conclusions reached through the process of communicative rationality across disciplines. For different purposes but in similar ways, SR (a) decenters our understanding of these texts—which I link with Adams's emphasis on teasing out interpretations and (b) encourages participation in what Habermas means by a "pragmatic logic of argumentation"—which relates to "making explicit . . . deep reasonings."

---

making deep reasonings public, by offering a forum, in which mutual learning of languages takes place, unpredictably, among friends, to which an open invitation is extended to those who are interested to participate." Adams, MDRP, 54.

31. Adams, MDRP, 56.

What is the risk of *not* having a practice where religious believers have an "extension" (Adams's word) or an outlet (my word) for what is akin to communicative rationality? Both Adams and Chouliaraki provide similar answers relating to the educational system, the media, and the nation-state. Chouliaraki claims that Habermas's philosophy shows deep concern for and wants to protect against both "questions of inequality" being turned "into the consumption of state services for the poor" and the manipulation of the media where "the moral force of suffering" gets replaced "with television spectacle." Similarly, Adams defends the claim that maintaining a practice that makes deep reasonings explicit and public protects against how "radio and television" tend to report on "religious attitudes" in ways that are "insufficiently informative about . . . religious attitudes"; he continues, "it is sometimes a wonder that such debates are considered at all worthwhile."[32] Adams goes a step further and offers the judgment: "Given the religious difficulties surrounding foreign policy, school education, and domestic and international law, it is surely a significant problem if the deep reasonings of religious traditions are not made public."[33] For me, this insight turns SR into a pedagogical call to arms (in the sense of a summons to engage in an activity or a practice in order to respond to a political crisis or political problems in general).

There are several implications concerning the strong link between Habermas's theory of communicative rationality and the practice of SR in terms of serving as corrections to subject-centered rationality.[34] This correction to

32. Adams, MDRP, 55.

33. Adams, MDRP, 55.

34. I attempt to perform what Adams claims about reflecting upon the practice of SR: "Scriptural reasoning is a 'fact': it actually happens. It can thus be investigated, and not only by its own

subject-centered rationality—his theory of communicative rationality—leads to Habermas's Discourse Ethics in order to maintain standards of goodness and truthfulness within the process of argumentation, conversation, and debate. Like religious traditions actively borrow from and build upon the traditional moral theories of deontology, utilitarianism, and virtue theory, communicative action relies on these moral theories as well. Discourse Ethics avoids the subject-centered rationality of Kant's deontological reasoning and takes a communication-based deontological approach by applying both the dignity test and the universalization test to the process of rational deliberation.

Observers and participants of SR will find these tests present at the table of study: the dignity test is found within the practice of SR when participants refuse to use other interlocutors as a means to their own intellectual end; the universalization test is found within the practice of SR—not through a process of consensus-building—but when participants treat the passages in front of them as sacred even when those passages come from texts that they might not consider sacred. (In this chapter, I simply assert this to be the case; in the conclusion, however, I provide more of an explanation of SR through the lens of Kant's categorical imperatives.) Through these two deontological tests (found in Kant's *Grounding for the Metaphysics of Morals*), SR maintains standards of goodness and truthfulness within the process of argumentation, conversation, and debate *with* members of other religious traditions and around objects of study considered sacred *by* those religious believers (participating in SR) and by religious traditions in general.

With these arguments, we arrive at a potential middle-ground between Habermas's refusal of friendship and

---

participants. Theoretical claims about it can be formulated, and not only by its participants." Adams, MDRP, 56.

vulnerability and Adams's over-confidence in friendship and vulnerability occurring within the practice of SR.[35] From a Habermasian perspective, participants who follow the dignity test in the process of communicative rationality should not be at risk for becoming friends because of the professional demands required for communicative rationality to work. From Adams's perspective, friendship seems inevitable within the practice of SR because making "deep reasonings public . . . foster[s] forms of collegial friendship by deepening relations between persons with respect to sacred texts."[36] Habermas prioritizes the goals of consensus and objectivity over "collegial friendship"[37] within the process of communicative rationality; recognizing that SR would be a completely different practice if consensus and objectivity were goals at all within the practice of SR (I challenge Adams on this point in the final section of this chapter), Adams opts for friendship as a possible goal—which results from deepening relationships but not as a substitute for showing other participants dignity.

My argument is that the dignity test within the context of SR might lead to friendship but reminds us of the high importance of treating other participants with dignity by refusing to make them merely a means to your own end. Furthermore, the universalization test provides a deontological rationale for a category such as vulnerability: participants make themselves vulnerable to the sacred texts of other religious traditions. (More on this in the conclusion.)

This seems like a middle-ground position between Adams and Habermas in the sense that vulnerability gets

35. I believe this middle-ground position best represents Mike Higton and Rachel Muers's textual representation of an SR session found in *TP*, ch. 9.

36. Adams, MDRP, 56.

37. See Adams, MDRP, 56.

postured toward the shared object of study rather than other people, but the dignity test keeps other participants in check to not manipulate and misuse the vulnerability displayed toward the object of study—the passages on the table from traditionally sacred texts. The comparison of the practice of SR with the process of communicative rationality teaches us that vulnerability can be directed toward objects of study while collegial or deep friendships might result from a practice or a process that intensely demands maintaining dignity between participants.

Habermas, Peirce, and SR

In his chapter in *The Promise of Scriptural Reasoning*, David Ford writes,

> At the beginning [of SR] the most influential theoretical contribution was Peter Ochs's use of C. S. Peirce's semiotics and relational logic, and that has continued to be a fruitful resource. . . . Nicholas Adams has engaged in critical discussion with Jürgen Habermas in dialogue with German Idealist philosophy from Kant to Schelling and Hegel . . .
>
> Such variety shows the capacity of scriptural interpretation to stimulate conceptual thinking in dialogue with pragmatism, idealism, phenomenology, social theory, legal theory, scientific theory, ethical theory, philosophy of language, philosophy of history, systems thinking, feminist theory, and hermeneutical philosophy. The very diversity also resists any theoretical overview—there can be no overall master theory where so many conceptual descriptions and analyses engage with each other. The intersection of such theoretical accounts also intensifies

> the conversation around scriptural texts and their implications.
>
> So the effort to "make deep reasonings public" . . . simultaneously leads deep into scriptures and deep into theories . . .[38]

So what is the difference between theorizing about SR in terms of Habermas's theory of communicative rationality rather than Peirce's pragmatism and semiotics? By answering this question and stating the difference between the two, I intend to simply keep the difference as *a* difference—and not to suggest a critique of Peirce's philosophy via Habermas's theory of communicative rationality. I also use this question to introduce more aspects of Peirce's pragmatism that relate to the practice of SR. The differences involve the relationship between consensus, the process of rationality, and Reality.[39]

On the one hand, Peirce's pragmatism seems to be simultaneously both underwhelming in terms of measuring success and overwhelming in terms of the ultimate goal.

38. Ford, "Interfaith Wisdom," 17–18.

39. I should note that Tom Rockmore sees more similarities between Habermas's theory of communication and Peirce's semiotics than what I suggest in this section; in his words: "Habermas regards Peirce as the first to see that knowledge relies on uncompelled and permanent consensus in the form of an ultimate answer to every scientific question. . . . Habermas's account of Peirce is intended to call attention to his [Peirce's] relation to Habermas's own version of the consensus theory of truth—[which] suggests an anti-Platonic, quasi-Kantian idealist claim according to which independent reality is not grasped as it is but is in some sense 'constructed' by the knower as a condition of knowledge. He [Habermas] goes on to argue that interpretation is based on consensus within the framework of tradition. . . . Habermas, who wisely denies the very idea that we in some way grasp mind-independent reality as it is, intends his claim as a revised form of the Socratic assumption, which functions normatively in the entire philosophical tradition, of dialogue as a source of truth." Rockmore, "Epistemological Promise of Pragmatism," 56.

In terms of the ultimate goal, Peirce thinks that the scientific process of rationality will result in Reality—in the metaphysical realist sense of Reality. In my judgment, SR cannot even begin to make promises about how its practice will someday come to the Reality of divine revelation. In terms of measuring success, Peirce has no category similar to Habermas's view of consensus as a way for us to judge whether the process works in the here and now. Peirce's pragmatism expects those within the scientific process of rationality to continually postpone judgment about the success of the process. Those who practice SR should fall in line with a Peircean postponement of judgment about the 'success' of SR study sessions.

Habermas's theory of communicative rationality, on the other hand, allows us to judge whether the process works in the here and now. Scriptural reasoners ought to become more comfortable—in specific settings—with claiming Habermasian consensus. While it has become quite commonplace amongst scriptural reasoners to say that Nicholas Adams demonstrates that the goal of SR is friendship and not consensus, I believe SR practitioners and theorists tend to overstate such a case.[40] Adams's actual published words are: "The process [of SR] cannot be rushed. That means that . . . the urgent need for consensus should not be allowed to force the pace of making deep reasonings public."[41] Adams rightly cautions that we should not be forcefully "making deep reasonings public" based upon the urgency of consensus, but this does not provide grounds to dismiss consensus wholesale within SR.[42] The consensus sought within SR is neither doctrinal agreement nor metaphysical finality but, rather, consensus concerning whether the practice ought to

40. See Adams, MDRP, 56.

41. Adams, MDRP, 56.

42. See Adams, MDRP, 56.

continue—perhaps at other places and in other times. This type of consensus follows from the dignity test within SR, in the sense that SR neither coerces nor forces the practice of SR onto its participants. Consensus merely follows from the ethical orientation of maintaining dignity taken toward one another within SR.

Furthermore, Habermas's theory of communicative rationality does not require thinking in terms of an ultimate goal as coming to agreement on Reality "in the long run" (as Peirceans are apt to say).[43] Putting this demand aside ought to free scriptural reasoners because if they do believe, with Peirce, that we will come to know the truth of Reality in the so-called long run then that ought to remain a tradition-specific enquiry—and not one that rests upon and within the practice of SR.[44] Habermas's theory of communicative rationality comes with expectations that are less overwhelming, in terms of coming to know Reality through the process of reasoning, and more helpful in the present moment for judging the success of the process of reasoning.

Both of these aspects aid reflections on the practice of SR quite well because Habermas's theory of communicative rationality (a) helps us recognize that continuing to pursue SR as a process of reasoning means that we have consensus that the practice remains worthy of our intellectual investment and (b) rids the potential (Peircean) assumption of thinking that SR will someday reveal the truth of Reality.[45]

---

43. There are three places where Habermas writes on Peirce's theories of Reality and Truth: *Knowledge and Human Interests*, ch. 5; *Legitimation Crisis*, 108; and *Truth and Justification*, ch. 2.

44. See Adams, *HT*, 238.

45. Morgan Elbot, Randy Friedman, Mark James, and Matthew Vaughan provided full responses to an earlier version of this chapter; I am grateful for their clarifications, disagreements, and questions in relation to what I argue here.

6

Friendship, Luck, Vulnerability

SR *after* Martha Nussbaum

> Our time is genuinely dangerous. As we have
> seen, many fears are rational, and appeals to
> fear have a role to play in a society that takes hu-
> man life seriously. Still, at this point, the balance
> has all too often shifted in the other direction,
> as irresponsibly manufactured fears threaten
> principles we should cling to and be proud of.
> To counteract the baneful tendency to narrow
> our sights in a focus on the all-important self, we
> need . . . to examine our choices to see whether
> they are selfish, ignoring the equal claims of oth-
> ers. And we need . . . , the inner spirit that must
> animate the search for consistency, if it is not to
> remain a hollow shell: we need, that is, the spirit
> of curiosity and friendship.[1]

Introduction

F riendship, luck, and vulnerability come up as themes
quite often within reflections on the practice of SR.

1. Nussbaum, *New Religious Intolerance*, 245.

Friendship is often contrasted with consensus—as in, SR leads to friendship and not consensus. Sometimes, the claim is made that whether an SR session works or not comes down to a matter of luck. Vulnerability relates to the task of "making deep reasonings public,"[2] discussed in chapter 5.

In this chapter, I bring these three themes together and test the claim that SR leads to friendship. What does it mean for an academic—indeed, a philosophical—practice to lead to friendship? Does such a standard put an undue burden on the practice of SR? If SR has no inherent teleology as a practice, then why make friendship an end or goal of SR?

My thesis for this chapter is that if scholars of SR continue to defend friendship as part and parcel of SR, then SR needs a very specific account of what friendship entails. Because of this, the majority of this chapter builds from and engages with Martha Nussbaum's account of *philia* in Aristotle's philosophy—which makes fragility, luck, and vulnerability necessary aspects of friendship. In this chapter, therefore, I offer SR scholars a theory of friendship that fits best for the kind of relationships that SR might be able to foster and nurture: friendships based upon *philia*, not *agape* (as some Christian theologians might assume serves as the most obvious type of love between friends of different religious traditions); friendships built on luck must remain fragile because of the peculiar sense of vulnerability involved in SR.[3]

2. See Adams, MDRP, 41–57.

3. In this chapter, I am trying to offer a similar argument concerning "the fragility of interreligious encounters" to the one found in Marianne Moyaert's *In Response to the Religious Other*.

Claims about Friendship within SR

At least three scholars of SR make claims about friendship—
Nicholas Adams, David Ford, and Daniel Hardy—all of
whose reflections on SR have been discussed in this book.[4]

First, David Ford means two things by the phrase
"not consensus but friendship."[5] The first part of the
phrase: "not consensus—that may happen, but it is more
likely that the conclusion will be a recognition of deep
differences."[6] The second part of the phrase: "hospitality
turning into friendship—each tradition values friendship,
and for it to happen now might be seen as the most tan-
gible anticipation of future peace."[7] While Ford makes
interesting claims about friendship, hospitality, and peace,
the phrase "each tradition values friendship" ought to be
judged as underdetermined and vague.[8] One of the questions addressed in this chapter, therefore, is: What does it
mean for religious traditions to value friendship?

Nicholas Adams echoes the phrasing of "not consensus but friendship" as a goal of SR. He puts it a bit
differently than Ford does: " . . . friendship rather than
agreement . . . : SR values friendships above consensus."[9]
Adams offers further distinctions: "In a context which aims
at consensus, disagreement is a problem to be overcome.
In a context which values friendship, disagreement is a

4. Sometimes, Peter Ochs makes distinctions concerning "American" vs. "British" tendencies within Christian theology (e.g., Ochs,
Another Reformation). If we follow that pattern, then it becomes clear
that thinking of SR as leading to friendship would be considered a
"British" tendency.

5. Ford, *CW*, 278.

6. Ford, *CW*, 278.

7. Ford, *CW*, 280.

8. See Ford, *CW*, 280.

9. Adams, MDRP, 52–53.

gift to be treasured. SR is a practice that sometimes treasures disagreement as a gift."[10] Because SR values friendship, disagreements are not problems to overcome within SR. These distinctions offer a bit more clarity than Ford does, and a difference between Adams and Ford concerns *who* values friendship: for Ford, religious traditions value friendship; for Adams, SR values friendship. The question shifts, then, to what does it mean for SR to *value* friendship? What kind of friendships can SR—a philosophical practice—foster, nurture, and value?

Adams also connects friendship with luck. After establishing SR as a practice relying on luck, he says, "there is one final point to be made about openness to luck."[11] This final point involves connections between friendship, future-orientation, and luck: "Friendship is made possible [within SR] . . . by being open to the future," and this openness to the future requires the exact same disposition as the "openness to luck" required within SR.[12] Within SR, friendships result from being open to the future *and* open to luck.

Daniel Hardy adds trust to Adams's and Ford's accounts of friendship within SR. Hardy writes, "the premium is not on consensus so much as friendship, and trust built through in-house or inter-traditional disagreements."[13] Ten pages later, however, Hardy questions whether these categories are sufficient for thinking about "the premium" of SR: "What kind of sociality is needed in SR . . . ? There . . . need[s] to be an ease with each other, and a high level of personal relationship, even in the presence of difference and disagreement. These are . . . 'friendship' and 'trust,'

---

10. Adams, MDRP, 54.

11. Adams, MDRP, 49.

12. Adams, MDRP, 49.

13. Hardy, PSR, 192.

but are those enough?"[14] Hardy's reflections on friendship ends with this skepticism, and my claim in this chapter is the following: While I would be content to share in Hardy's skepticism about the category of friendship within SR, for those SR practitioners and theorists who wish to maintain friendship as one of the ends or goals of SR, then Martha Nussbaum's account of *philia*—found in Aristotle's philosophy—is the version of friendship that ought to be adopted for and within SR.

Nussbaum on Friendship and *Philia*

In *The Fragility of Goodness*, Nussbaum theorizes about the connections between friendship, luck, and vulnerability. If SR practitioners and theorists wish to make claims about friendship and luck, as Adams does, then Nussbaum's account of *philia* offers the most wisdom for what such friendships can and should look like. This section makes that case.

Nussbaum does not allow her readers to call relationships based upon *philia* friendships. She explains why:

> [W]e are not going to follow the usual practice of translating *philia* as "friendship" [or] *philos* as friend. . . . The first reason is extensional: *philia* includes many relationships that would not be classified as friendships. . . . Furthermore, our "friendship" can suggest a relationship that is weak in affect relative to some other relationship, as in the expression "just friends."[15]

While I agree with her warnings about equating friendship with *philia*, in this chapter I continue to use "the usual

14. Hardy, PSR, 202.
15. Nussbuam, *Fragility of Goodness*, 354.

141

practice of translating *philia* as 'friendship'" and "*philos* as friend" because I believe we can maintain that tradition of thought *and* acknowledge Nussbaum's clarifications with what *philia* does not mean.[16] *Philia* includes neither the "many relationships that would not be classified as friend-ships" nor relationships that might be considered as "'just friends.'"[17] Therefore, what Nussbaum considers relation-ships based upon *philia* is what I apply as the potential for friendship within SR.

According to Nussbaum, thinking about friendship requires starting with the category of luck within ancient philosophy. Nussbaum writes, "We are asking . . . about the power of luck or fortune to influence the goodness and praiseworthiness of a human life."[18] In other words, the question of friendship can never be divorced from luck. Why is this? Because friendship, in its "very nature," represents a "contingent relationship . . . between elements in the world"—which means "luck from the world will be required not just for their adequate expression but for their very existence."[19] Friendships require luck.

When luck in fact leads to friendships, then what do these relationships look like? First, friendship "requires . . . mutuality in affection; it requires separateness and a mutual respect for separateness; it requires mutual well-wishing for the other's own sake and . . . mutual benefitting in action."[20] With the emphasis on difference and disagreement within SR, this aspect of developing friendships fits quite well with what relationships look like within the practice of SR. SR

16. See Nussbuam, *Fragility of Goodness*, 354.
17. See Nussbuam, *Fragility of Goodness*, 354.
18. Nussbaum, *Fragility of Goodness*, 319.
19. Nussbaum, *Fragility of Goodness*, 343–44.
20. Nussbaum, *Fragility of Goodness*, 355.

involves differences between participants but also requires a "mutual respect" in regards to those differences.[21]

Second, friendship requires knowing one another. Nussbaum treats this as a step beyond "mutuality in affection."[22] She writes that friendship

> must be distinguished from the sort of mutual admiration that could obtain between people who had no knowledge at all of one another. These people know each other, feel emotion for one another, wish and act well towards one another, and know that these relationships of thought, emotion, and action obtain between them.[23]

Within the practice of SR, it seems a reasonable inference from the fact of "wish[ing] and act[ing] well towards one another" to the reality of "feel[ing] emotions for one another."[24] However, it certainly would be wrong to say that everyone who practices SR "feel[s] emotion for one another."[25]

Third, Nussbaum connects friendship with vulnerability. Friendship means a high amount of vulnerability "to happenings in the world."[26] What are "sources of that vulnerability"?[27] Nussbaum offers two answers to this question: (a) finding a friend, itself, requires an intense amount of vulnerability because of having to submit oneself to "the luck of finding . . . one to value"; and (b) "two [friends] must find themselves able to trust one another."[28]

21. See Nussbaum, *Fragility of Goodness*, 355.

22. See Nussbaum, *Fragility of Goodness*, 355.

23. Nussbaum, *Fragility of Goodness*, 355.

24. See Nussbaum, *Fragility of Goodness*, 355.

25. See Nussbaum, *Fragility of Goodness*, 355.

26. Nussbaum, *Fragility of Goodness*, 359.

27. Nussbaum, *Fragility of Goodness*, 359.

28. Nussbaum, *Fragility of Goodness*, 359.

By trust, Nussbaum means the ability "to receive one another's expressions . . . without suspicion, jealousy, of fearful self-protectiveness."[29] (She clarifies her use of suspicion as "The suspicion of hypocrisy and falsity."[30]) In relation to fear, Nussbaum claims that friendship "requires a kind of openness and receptivity that is incompatible with fear."[31] As a practice, SR simply does not work if participants are fearful and suspicious of one another.

A critique of Nussbaum's account of *philia* claims that her theory of friendship cannot and does not apply to religious believers—particularly, to Christians and Jews. This critique comes from Stanley Hauerwas and Charles Pinches, in their essay "Friendship and Fragility," and it raises helpful questions for applying Nussbaum's account of *philia* to the relationships formed within SR. According to Hauerwas and Pinches, Christians and Jews can go along with Nussbaum's connection between friendship and vulnerability to some extent but not her development of luck. Christians and Jews do not see the world in terms of luck because such a concept plays into a pagan notion of chaos; rather, Christians and Jews recognize God as ordering creation despite human beings not always being able to see such order.

They go on to argue, however, that the Christian tradition has an altogether different take on *philia* than Nussbaum offers. Thereby, Christianity reformulates the relationship between friendship and vulnerability. Applying it to SR, Hauerwas and Pinches would say that the kind of friendships possible in SR are best described as *agape* instead of *philia*. How does their argument arrive at this conclusion?

29. Nussbaum, *Fragility of Goodness*, 359.

30. Nussbaum, *Fragility of Goodness*, 359.

31. Nussbaum, *Fragility of Goodness*, 359.

Vulnerability becomes intensified in their argument against Nussbaum's account of *philia*. They write,

> [D]istinctly Christian love [is] communally given; it is a love in which individual persons share, rather than a love one of them possesses or . . . gives by himself. Or, to place *agape* in relation to the *philia* [found in Nussbaum's account], one might say that *philia* in the Christian church forms Christians to embody the love . . . described as *agape*. Yet in saying so we must hold tight to the Aristotelian insight. For it is not that . . . Christians are formed by *philia* to become individuals who [then] individually practice *agape*. Rather, it is that we are formed by *philia* in the church to become a community which in its corporate life in the world loves the world in the manner of *agape*, whose practice it has learned in seeking to conform itself to the God who is in Christ.[32]

Vulnerability becomes intensified in this argument in the sense that neither *agape* nor *philia* are loves that are possessed by an individual but always "communally given" and, therefore, always already shared between people.[33]

To the extent that Hauerwas and Pinches are willing to play the game on the terms of Aristotle and Nussbaum, they articulate a process of the relationship between *agape* and *philia*. This process begins with *philia* as determined and embodied within Christian community, and the *philia* nurtured within Christian community leads to *agape* with those outside of Christian community—in short, non-Christian believers. At no point in this process are *agape* and *philia* possessed by individuals where an individual

32. Hauerwas and Pinches, "Friendship and Fragility," 82.

33. See Hauerwas and Pinches, "Friendship and Fragility," 82.

willingly offers *agape* and *philia* to others. Rather, non-Christians are the recipients of *agape* from Christian community—which manifests itself in encounters between individuals, but Hauerwas and Pinches make clear in the beginning of the essay that there are no "personal" relationships possible independent of the politics of communal formations.[34]

Returning to how this argument applies to SR: Christian participants in SR cannot have relationships with Jews and Muslims based upon *philia* but only based on *agape*—which is best translated and understood as charity. They (Christian participants) do so *not because of the practice of SR but because* agape *is the name for the excess of love in relation to the* philia *of Christian community*. Christian community leads to friendships based on *agape*; the practice and relational dynamics of SR do not lead to such friendships. This seems to be the most reasonable conclusion about SR that can be inferred from Hauerwas's and Pinches's argument.

Perhaps more importantly than the cause of friendship concerns the type of friendship: *agape* or *philia*? Hauerwas and Pinches are adamant that Christians cannot and do not have friendships based upon *philia* with non-Christians "in the world."[35] They can, however, cultivate friendships based upon *agape*—and, again, the best translation for this type of love is charity. These kinds of friendships do not skirt the issue of vulnerability but intensify vulnerability because *agape* has to become a constant and real possibility: Christians never know who might become their friends, at least when it comes to friendships based upon charity. In their words: "Christian community is continually required

34. See Hauerwas and Pinches, "Friendship and Fragility," 70–74.
35. See Hauerwas and Pinches, "Friendship and Fragility," 82.

to offer hospitality to the stranger,"[36] and Christians are "challenged to sustain and nourish their friendships in the midst of a community that does not protect them from the stranger."[37] At the heart of this claim is the Aristotelian insight that human beings only learn proper friendship from virtuous models of friendship. Hauerwas and Pinches reduce the possibility for this model down to Jesus Christ, which for them is all that it means to talk about a *Christian* view of friendship: for Christians, Jesus Christ becomes the singular model for friendship. Once this premise is in place, then it becomes clearer what it means to say that vulnerability is intensified—not lessened—with friendships based upon *agape*. Christians learn "friendship from Christ," Hauerwas and Pinches declare, "who welcomed children, prostitutes, and Samaritans, and who commands them [his followers] to do likewise."[38]

On the one hand, the argument presented by Hauerwas and Pinches might be seen as an upgrade within the Christian tradition. Famously, Søren Kierkegaard made a strong case for why Christians cannot have friends at all—only neighbors and enemies, both of whom must be loved in the same way (*agape*).[39] For Kierkegaard, the command of *agape* removes the possibility of friendship for Christians. At the least, therefore, Hauerwas and Pinches allow Christians to call relationships based upon *agape* "friendships."[40]

36. Hauerwas and Pinches, "Friendship and Fragility," 83.

37. Hauerwas and Pinches, "Friendship and Fragility," 84.

38. Hauerwas and Pinches, "Friendship and Fragility," 84.

39. See Kierkegaard, "'You Shall Love Your *Neighbor*,'" 233–47.

40. However, in my judgment, Hauerwas and Pinches dismiss Kierkegaard's argument too quickly when they say that Kierkegaard "struggled with the '*tension*' . . . presume[d] [to] exist between friendship and 'Christian love.'" They explain further, "Behind this tension stands a presumption: there is some solitary Christian self who alternatively enters into (chooses to enter into) relations which are *philia*

However, on the other hand, it seems that Nussbaum's understanding of *philia* better applies to the types of relationships formed and found within the practice of SR than Hauerwas and Pinches's notion of *agape* does. I say this mostly because I think her account of fragility, luck, and vulnerability fit with what tends to happen in SR rather than simply saying that the friendships that seem to be formed in SR *really are the result* of prior religious formation(s). In other words, Hauerwas and Pinches claim to know too much ahead of time. They offer an *a priori* account of friendship—where friendships *always* result from one's formation within their religious community and *never* result from practices occurring within the world. For friendship to result from practices within the world, one has to have some luck—which makes one vulnerable to others and to those practices. For me, this better describes SR: SR is a practice within the world comprised of believers from multiple religious traditions, and it relies on luck to go well as a practice and requires an intense amount of vulnerability from its participants. Christian participants can explain or justify their willingness to be vulnerable based on the model of Jesus Christ, but such vulnerability—if truly vulnerable—means that how it goes totally depends upon the relational dynamics within the practice. What is the one word we tend to use for how it goes totally depending upon relational dynamics? Luck.

Nussbaum offers an implicit response to Hauerwas's and Pinches's criticisms in her later book, *The New Religious Intolerance*. In that book, Nussbaum turns to the Sermon on the Mount as a way to think through what she calls "civic friendship."[41] She connects Jesus Christ's words—"And why

---

or relations which are *agape*." Hauerwas and Pinches, "Friendship and Fragility," 82.

41. See Nussbaum, *New Religious Intolerance*, 100–187.

do you take note of the mote that is in your brother's eye, but pay no attention to the large plank that is in your own eye? Or how will you say to your brother, 'Let me take that mote out of your own eye' while, behold, a plank is in your own eye"—with Socrates' conversations with Euthyphro and Laches.[42] She articulates how this wisdom from "Christian ethics" (her phrase) contains both a negative and a positive insight about human relationships.[43] The negative insight: with Socrates, Jesus's words warn us about committing "selfish inconsistencies."[44] In his conversations with Euthyphro and Laches, Socrates leaves us with this negative insight and does not add a positive one. Jesus, however, warns us about committing "selfish inconsistencies" but also gives us a positive insight about human relationships—which leads to Nussbaum's account of "civic friendships."[45] Jesus's positive insight is that human beings need not be imprisoned, stuck, or trapped by "the error of making a special case for themselves."[46] Some might read Jesus's words as limiting the judgmental aspects of human nature, but Nussbaum reads it differently: Jesus wants to free us from the tendency to make a special case for ourselves. Once freed from this tendency, human beings can enter into and enjoy "civic friendships"—which involves what seems to be "the bare bones of friendship."[47] She lists

> curiosity, listening, responsiveness, a willingness
> to acknowledge a full life and world . . . outside

42. Matt 7:3–4; quoted in Nussbaum, *New Religious Intolerance*, 100.

43. See Nussbaum, *New Religious Intolerance*, 100–101.

44. See Nussbaum, *New Religious Intolerance*, 98–100.

45. See Nussbaum, *New Religious Intolerance*, 100–187.

46. Nussbaum, *New Religious Intolerance*; this phrasing is used throughout pages 100–187.

47. Nussbaum, *Fragility of Goodness*, 187.

149

ourselves. Friendship is rarely uncritical, and friends may well differ in their evaluations and argue, sometimes fiercely. But to remain friends, they must . . . see the situation from the other point of view. They must [continue to] avoid the error of making a special case [for] themselves.[48]

Nussbaum's description of "civic friendship" accurately and wisely captures the kind of relationships that SR make possible in SR's best version of itself—especially her emphasis on how "civic friendships" allow for both fierce argument and seeing "from the other point of view."[49] In the case of SR, seeing "the other point of view" is not necessarily about seeing *the world* from other points of view but about seeing *the text* "from the other point of view."[50]

Additionally, Nussbaum claims that "civic friendships" model an alternative to "seeing the world through the narcissism of anxiety."[51] How do "civic friendships" become such a model?[52] Because they perform "a triple task": "first . . . , to lure people's imaginations and entice them to care about the people" they encounter in the world; second, "to convince" those who tend to act with "the narcissism of anxiety" that "the people there"—those whom they encounter in the world—"are not actually disgusting or evil"; and third, to convince those who tend to act with "the narcissism of anxiety" that "the people there"—those whom they encounter in the world—are "deserving of friendship and respect."[53] Nussbaum points toward individual authors who model

48. Nussbaum, *New Religious Intolerance*, 187.

49. Nussbaum, *New Religious Intolerance*, 187.

50. Nussbaum, *New Religious Intolerance*, 187.

51. Nussbaum, *New Religious Intolerance*, 187.

52. Nussbaum, *New Religious Intolerance*, 187.

53. Nussbaum, *New Religious Intolerance*, 186–87.

"civic friendship" through their writing.[54] As a practice, how-ever, SR can serve as a concrete model for civic friendship. Those who tend to see "the world through the narcissism of anxiety"[55] can be shown, through the practice of SR, what it looks like to be freed from such narcissism. This seems a more humble and realistic promise than the promise of "peace" found in Peter Ochs's description and reflections on the practice of SR,[56] but "civic friendships" also could be understood as a means to the greater end of "peace" among the members of the Abrahamic traditions.[57]

Conclusion

I read Martha Nussbaum's *New Religious Intolerance* as providing two arguments that implicitly respond to the criticisms of *The Fragility of Goodness* made by Stanley Hauerwas and Charles Pinches. I continue to believe that the issues raised by Nussbaum, Hauerwas, and Pinches remain so critical for understanding friendship and vul-nerability within the practice of SR. I conclude with an additional third point that brings together arguments and insights from *The Fragility of Goodness* with *The New Reli-gious Intolerance* in ways helpful for SR.

First, Hauerwas and Pinches claim that one of the problems with *The Fragility of Goodness* concerns how Nussbaum mistakenly distinguishes between "personal" and "political" friendships and then shows favor toward "personal" friendships.[58] Their critique is that she claims

54. See Nussbaum, *New Religious Intolerance*, 186–87.

55. Nussbaum, *New Religious Intolerance*, 187.

56. See Geddes, "Peacemaking among the Abrahamic Faiths," 90–102.

57. See Nussbaum, *New Religious Intolerance*, 100–187.

58. See Hauerwas and Pinches, "Friendship and Fragility," 70–88.

to be following Aristotle's moral reasoning, but Aristotle never imagined—indeed, would not be able to make sense of—the notion of a "personal" friendship in the sense of a non-political friendship.[59] In *The New Religious Intolerance*, Nussbaum implicitly responds to this critique by (a) using the words "civic" and "political" interchangeably when discussing "civic friendships," (b) avoiding any distinction between "civic friendship" and "personal friendships," and (c) arguing that "civic friendships" serve the common good in the best ways possible in the twenty-first century—a century so far defined and determined, Nussbaum contends, by a "new religious intolerance."[60] SR helps citizens overcome both old versions of religious intolerance and the new religious intolerance. Contrary to what some might infer: what this overcoming looks like, following Nussbaum, is not simply a shift from intolerance to tolerance but a shift from *xenophobia* to the cultivation of friendship. I take this claim to be at the heart of those SR practitioners and theorists who argue that SR leads to friendship. My contribution to this argument involves offering Nussbuam's wisdom for what these friendships look like and to call the kind of friendships cultivated within SR "civic" or "political" friendships.[61]

Second, Nussbaum's interpretation and use of Matthew 7:3–4 offers an alternative account—alternative to that of Hauerwas and Pinches's emphasis on *agape* as the only type of friendship possible between Christians and non-Christians—of what *Christian* friendships might look like. According to Nussbaum, Jesus's words in Matthew 7 demonstrate how human beings can be freed from the tendency to make a special case for ourselves. Once freed from

59. See Hauerwas and Pinches, "Friendship and Fragility," 70–88.

60. See Nussbaum, *New Religious Intolerance*, 100–187.

61. See Nussbaum, *New Religious Intolerance*, 100–187.

this tendency, human beings can enter into and enjoy "civic friendships."[62] These "civic friendships" fall in line closer to Nussbaum's use of *philia* in *The Fragility of Goodness* than to Hauerwas and Pinches's use of *agape* in "Friendship and Fragility." In the next chapter, I develop as fully as possible the role of *philia* within SR.

Third, Nussbaum makes two arguments—neither one yet mentioned in this chapter—that I highlight now because I am confident that SR achieves both of them. Although I remain skeptical about the claim that SR leads to friendship—and if SR theorists wish to make this claim, then this chapter ought to be perceived as my gifting Nussbaum's reflections on friendship to SR for what such a claim can and should mean—I am confident that what SR has achieved and continues to achieve is found in these two arguments.

In *The Fragility of Goodness*, Nussbaum writes,

> [A] fact of human psychology: it is difficult for each of us to see our own life clearly and without bias, assessing its patterns of action and commitment. Often we lack awareness of our own faults, because we are blinded by partiality and by involvement in our own feelings and concerns.[63]

How do we avoid this difficulty? By "improving self-criticism . . . , sharpening [our] judgment," and tracking "person[s] similar to ourselves in character and aspiration, someone [singular or plural] whom we can identify to ourselves as 'another oneself' for the purposes of this scrutiny."[64] SR provides a context and setting, an exercise and practice, a time and place for all three of these to

---

62. See Nussbaum, *New Religious Intolerance*, 100–101.

63. Nussbaum, *Fragility of Goodness*, 364.

64. Nussbaum, *Fragility of Goodness*, 364.

occur—each of which correlate with friendship, luck, and vulnerability:

> *Vulnerability*—"improving self-criticism":[65] SR achieves this through making participants vulnerable to others by offering interpretations of their own sacred texts and sacred texts belonging to other religious traditions.

> *Luck*—"sharpening judgment":[66] with some luck, SR achieves this by the constant back-and-forth in relation to participants agreeing and disagreeing about what the texts say, participants holding each other accountable to stay within the bounds of the passages in front of them, and raising critical questions that help participants read their own sacred texts in new ways but also build their confidence in reading sacred texts from other religious traditions. (I echo the claim mentioned in the opening paragraph of this chapter that whether an SR session works or not comes down to a matter of luck.)

> *Friendship*—tracking "person[s] similar to ourselves in character and aspiration, someone [singular or plural] whom we can identify to ourselves as 'another oneself' for the purposes of this scrutiny":[67] SR achieves this, not because the participants are like-minded in terms of academic disciplines and religious affiliation (which they are not), but because they enter into a practice centered around reading traditionally sacred texts together without knowing what the results will be.

---

65. Nussbaum, *Fragility of Goodness*, 364.
66. Nussbaum, *Fragility of Goodness*, 364.
67. Nussbaum, *Fragility of Goodness*, 364.

This last point leads to the second argument I wish to high-light—this time from *The New Religious Intolerance.*

According to Nussbaum, in the twenty-first century (what she labels as a "dangerous" time), people need to find ways to get outside of themselves and their own beliefs. From my perspective, SR provides a practice that allows people to make that particular move—getting outside themselves and their own beliefs—as well encouraging others to get outside of themselves and their own beliefs. We do not have to be imprisoned, stuck, or trapped by our own egos; SR offers a way out, and this way out involves nurturing a "spirit of curiosity and friendship"![68]

68. Nussbaum, *New Religious Intolerance*, 245. For context, see the full paragraph placed at the beginning of this chapter.

Part 4

The *Inter-Religious* Aspect of Scriptural Reasoning

In chapter 7, I build on the argument of chapter 6 concerning *philia* and take the next step to showing that SR is a practice that nurtures *xenophilia*—which means that chapter 7 contributes to the argument that SR is a purposeful practice. The most obvious modern philosopher to engage with on *xenophilia* is G. W. F. Hegel—whose philosophy of religion can be interpreted as how being religious means or requires loving the otherness of strangers or loving the differences of others.

7

Is Scriptural Reasoning an Inter-faith Dialogue?

SR *after* Hegel

The question of what kind of dialogue or engagement best describes the practice of Scriptural Reasoning has been asked by some since SR has been a practice, and it certainly remains a question that drives my own interest in and passion for the practice. Is it an *inter-religious* dialogue—better put as an inter-religious trialogue—between members of the Jewish, Christian, and Islamic religions?[1] Since it has been limited to these three religious traditions for most of its history, is SR better described as an internal

1. This is what Marianne Moyaert considers the best label for SR; see Moyaert, "Scriptural Reasoning as Inter-Religious Dialogue," 64–86. I have no problem with Moyaert's description of SR as an "inter-religious dialogue" and will continue to label it as such in my everyday conversations. The purpose of the present chapter is to challenge the notion of SR as an inter-faith dialogue, and the purpose of the next chapter involves teasing out calling SR an inter-hope exercise or practice *in addition to* calling it an inter-religious dialogue on the terms of Moyaert.

conversation for those who share covenant with Abraham?[2] Is it an *inter-faith* dialogue or practice between members of the Abrahamic traditions?[3] Or is SR best thought of as a type of cosmopolitan universalism that nurtures conversation for the sake of conversation?[4]

In this chapter, I think through the possibility of SR as an inter-faith dialogue or practice. Turning to the work of the German philosopher G. W. F. Hegel (1770–1831), I negate the question: Should SR be described as an inter-faith dialogue? My negation concerns protecting the word "faith" and the role of faith in regard to the practitioners of SR. In other words, I argue that the concept of inter-faith dialogue actually downplays the place of faith within that dialogue. To make this argument, I borrow and build from the interpretation of Hegel's philosophy of religion found in Andrew Shanks's defense of *xenophilia*—how faith ought to lead to a love for the other without making the otherness of the other less other.[5]

2. For a defense of this description, see Greggs, "Peoples of the Covenants."

3. This is what David Ford considers the best label for SR; see Ford, "Interfaith Wisdom," 1–22.

4. Stanley Hauerwas makes the judgment that it is a mistake to think of SR in these terms. He writes, "I think there is a danger in interpreting the work of Scriptural Reasoning in large 'good guy terms' that doesn't do justice to the significance of the practice itself. By 'good guy terms' I mean that we celebrate what wonderful people we are because we respect one another sufficiently to be reading scripture together in the same room. Such a perception is to give a humanistic and cosmopolitan narrative to the activity that I think betrays anyone who has been shaped by Peter [Ochs]'s understanding of Scriptural Reasoning." Hauerwas, "Conversation with Stanley Hauerwas on Peace and War after Scriptural Reasoning."

5. In addition to following Nussbaum's account of *philia*, this chapter can be read as a follow-up to my critique of the *xenophobia* found in American Evangelical Christianity (see Goodson, *Dark Years?*, ch. 7); that chapter was critical and deconstructive whereas

First, I explain the pertinent aspects of Hegel's philosophy of religion—pertinent to the practice of SR. Second, I demonstrate the problems of the concept or phrase "inter-faith dialogue." Third, I argue that SR provides a "new space" for shifting from the fearfulness of *xenophobia* to the hopefulness of *xenophilia*.[6] I conclude by separating myself a bit from Shanks's interpretation of Hegel's philosophy of religion.

Faith in Hegel's Philosophy of Religion

Writing on Hegel's philosophy of religion remains quite a difficult task.[7] Turning to Hegel's philosophy of religion, however, is not new for thinking about the practice of SR. In 2015, the *Journal of Scriptural Reasoning* published a set of papers under the section heading of "Philosophical Theology after Hegel."[8] In her contribution to that section of *JSR*, Molly Farneth reflects upon what Hegel expects from "inter-religious" encounters (note that she does not use the phrase "inter-faith dialogue")—going as far as suggesting that Hegel envisions the possibility of *more than* inter-religious encounters but actual inter-religious communities:

> [Inter-religious practices] require . . . the relinquishment of the pretense to a God's-eye view and, in its place, the recognition of mutual

---

this chapter offers up Hegel's philosophy of religion as a constructive and faithful way forward past the sin(s) of *xenophobia*.

6. See Shanks, *Hegel vs. "Inter-Faith Dialogue"*, 64.

7. I am especially grateful for Jackson Lashier's feedback on the argument made in this particular section.

8. The essays were written in order to celebrate and honor the publication of Nicholas Adams's book on Hegel's philosophy of religion entitled *Eclipse of Grace*.

authority and accountability. Confession and forgiveness play the role that they do in Hegel's account of reconciliation because life among people who have abandoned the God's-eye view of truth, but who insist on making truth-claims nevertheless, are bound to disagree, to err, to require forgiveness, and to be able to offer it. If we care about truth, conflict is a given, but reciprocal recognition and reconciliation remain possibilities in both thought and practice. We learn to endure difference, even to recognize the ways in which we are constituted by it, as we give up a logic of either indifference or opposition and cultivate a logic of distinction-in-inseparable-relation. A Hegelian approach to interreligious encounter, to life in the religiously diverse community, acknowledges the perpetuity of difference and our endurance of it in right relations of tolerance and reciprocal recognition.[9]

I agree with Farneth's reflections on Hegel and what interreligious encounters might look like based upon arguments found in the *Phenomenology of Spirit*, and I wish to apply more explicitly Hegel's work to the particular practice of SR. To achieve this, I focus on what Hegel means by faith, reason and universal reason, and truth (also mentioned by Farneth).

What does Hegel mean by faith? His answers to this question evolve throughout his philosophical career. His answer in 1802 (in *Faith and Knowledge*) is:

> In true faith the whole sphere of finitude, of being-something-on-one's-own-account, the sphere of sensibility sinks into nothing before the thinking . . . of the eternal . . . [A]ll the midges of subjectivity are burned to death in

9. Farneth, "God, Community, and the Endurance of Difference."

this consuming fire, and *the very* consciousness
of this surrender and nullification is nullified.[10]

In 1802, Hegel defines faith as what brings together subjectivity with "the eternal."[11]

When Ochs, Hardy, and Ford claim that SR allows its participants to fully bring their own faith to the table—and all that is asked that might not be consistent with one's tradition is to treat the sacred texts of others also as Scripture *for the sake of the practice*—it sounds (at least to me) that they are making a Hegelian point about the practice of SR: SR works as a practice if and only if the participants perform "being-something-on-one's-own-account."[12] In other words, faith enhances the practice of SR because to be faithful is to become more than who one is in one's natural state. In Hegel's words: "the midges of subjectivity are burned to death in this consuming fire," but the need to nullify and surrender one's self becomes "nullified."[13] Faith does not decrease one's humanity or personhood but enhances it. The Ochs/Hardy/Ford claim about SR involves how faith—participants being fully Christian, Jewish, or Muslim—enhances the practice.

With the first publication of the *Phenomenology of Spirit* in 1807, Hegel describes faith as unproblematically both intensely subjective and extensively universal. By which he means faith (as claimed in *Faith and Knowledge*) increases who one is internally and subjectively;[14] faith also

10. Hegel, *Faith and Knowledge*, 141.

11. See Hegel, *Faith and Knowledge*, 141.

12. Hegel, *Faith and Knowledge*, 141.

13. See Hegel, *Faith and Knowledge*, 141. I should note that this argument can be interpreted as congruent with the New Testament claim that losing one's self really means gaining one's self.

14. "Faith is thereby pure consciousness of the *essence*, which is to say, of *simple inwardness*, and *is* therefore thought—and thought

empowers—note that power and virtue are sometimes interchangeable—one to access "universal reason."[15] In other words, faith intensely affirms and enhances the self while simultaneously moving the self beyond itself to participate extensively in universal reason.

For instance, Christians often use the locution of "I have faith in God." Hegel wants us to break this down as simultaneously moving in two directions: faith moves toward the "I" in a particular way, and faith means movement toward "God" in another way (what he calls "universal reason").[16] The first movement affirms persons in their convictions, individuality, and subjectivity; the second movement means that persons of faith must become and remain open to that which is greater or beyond one's self—what Hegel continually calls the work of the Spirit. For Hegel, genuine faith does not limit one's perspective but in fact opens a person up to "universal reason" as determined by and given through the Spirit.[17] For Hegel, this is what it means for the faithful to participate in the work of the Spirit.

Within the practice of SR, to fully bring one's faith to the table means asserting one's self as a committed Muslim, Jew, or Christian but also requires an openness in affirming the religious identities of others at the table. This type of *openness* becomes part and parcel of Hegel's understanding of faith. Andrew Shanks explains, "By 'Spirit' Hegel . . . basically means that which true Faith renders explicit;

---

becomes the chief moment in the nature of faith." Hegel, *Phenomenology of Spirit*, 321.

15. "[Faith] is thereby pure *being-for-itself*, not as *this individual*, but rather as the self which is *universal* . . . , as a restless movement which attacks and permeates the *motionless essence* of the *thing at issue*." Hegel, *Phenomenology of Spirit*, 321.

16. See Hegel, *Phenomenology of Spirit*, 321.

17. See Hegel, *Phenomenology of Spirit*, 321.

the otherwise implicit, universal impulse towards perfect truth-as-openness."[18] Shanks capitalizes what Hegel means by "Faith" throughout his book, in order to distinguish what Christians tend to mean by "faith" in their ordinary language—the ordinary usage of the word "faith" is up for constant criticism from Shanks. In their ordinary usage of "faith," Shanks thinks, Christians tend toward meaning both a "boasting" about one's self—"look how faithful a Christian I am!"—and a following of the herd: "The judgment of the herd is in terms of the tick-box, checklist fulfillment of certain readily achievable minimum requirements, assuring one's membership within the said herd."[19]

What Christians should mean by the word "faith"— the sense of faith that Shanks capitalizes throughout his book—should fall in line with Hegel's use of it. What does Hegel mean by faith? Shanks's answer: "*essentially* a relationship with God made manifest in and through a certain quality of sympathetic moral open-mindedness toward one's neighbors."[20] This is the version of "Faith" that Shanks capitalizes throughout his book, *Hegel vs. "Inter-Faith Dialogue"*.[21] My claim is that the type of faith envisioned by Ochs/Hardy/Ford for SR to work as a practice must be a type of faith much closer to that of "Faith"—a faith that requires openness—than "faith"—a faith that means both "boasting" about one's self and "following" the "judgment of the herd . . . in terms of the tick-box, checklist fulfillment of certain readily achievable minimum requirements, assuring one's membership within the said herd."[22]

18. Shanks, *Hegel vs. "Inter-Faith Dialogue"*, 49.

19. Shanks, *Hegel vs. "Inter-Faith Dialogue"*, 35.

20. Shanks, *Hegel vs. "Inter-Faith Dialogue"*, 3.

21. See Shanks, *Hegel vs. "Inter-Faith Dialogue"*, 3.

22. Shanks, *Hegel vs. "Inter-Faith Dialogue"*, 35.

With his lectures on the philosophy of religion, given twenty years after the first publication of *Phenomenology of Spirit* in 1827, Hegel explicitly connects faith with truth.[23] He says,

> The expression "faith," however, is used chiefly for the certainty that there is a God; and it is indeed used inasmuch as we do not have insight into the necessity of this content. . . . [T]o that extent we say that "faith" is something subjective, as opposed to which the knowledge of necessity is termed objective. For this reason . . . , we speak of "faith in God"—according to ordinary linguistic usage—because we have no immediate sensible intuition of God. But we do believe in God, and to that extent we have the certainty that God is. . . . The genuine content of a religion has for its verification the witness of one's own spirit, that this content conforms to the nature of my spirit and satisfies the needs of my spirit. My spirit knows itself, it knows its essence—that, too, is an immediate knowledge, it is the absolute verification of the eternally true, the simple and true definition of this certainty that is called faith. This certainty (and faith with

23. Nicholas Adams warns, "We do not have Hegel's *Lectures on the Philosophy of Religion*. Instead, we have some manuscripts and some editions based on now-lost manuscripts, and we have a carefully researched German edition that makes the best of a frustrating situation. Anyone citing Hegel's *Lectures on the Philosophy of Religion* is thus not citing Hegel, but citing a text that bears some relation (with luck, a close one) to what Hegel delivered in Berlin all those years ago." Adams, *Eclipse of Grace*, 169. When I cite Hegel's *Lectures on the Philosophy of Religion* in this chapter, I claim to be citing Hegel—which I choose to do for the sake of keeping the prose as clear as possible.

> it) enters into an antithesis with thought, and
> with truth in general.[24]

When it comes to passages like this one, where Hegel pits faith against truth, Shanks points out that Hegel's assumed target is not "truth-as-openness" but "truth-as-correctness."[25] I agree with Shanks's clarificatory move here—which means that we can use it to clarify the end of this passage: "faith . . . enters into an antithesis with thought, and with truth in general" when truth is assumed and understood to be about possession instead of dispossession.[26]

With the distinction concerning possession vs. dispossession, we have arrived at one of my big reveals about what Hegel contributes to thinking in relation to the significance of SR. When it comes to concerns about inter-faith or inter-religious dialogue, there seems to be two main ones: (a) my possession of the truth will clash with what others believe or think, and (b) religious differences should not be affirmed if one is really true to their own faith. Hegel teaches us that both concerns are misguided, and SR can be a practice that embodies and performs Hegel's insights. Concerning (a): to be faithful does not mean to have a special claim on truth— to possess truths that others do not possess—but means to *dispossess the truth*: to dispossess what one thinks is true so that one becomes possessed by the truth. According to David Ford, this sense of truth cannot and should not be divorced from the wisdom found in and offered by the *sacred texts of all three Abrahamic traditions*.[27] Concerning (b): Hegel predicts that what will become the problem within the modern world is not how to achieve communities and

---

24. Hegel, *Lectures on the Philosophy of Religion*, 136–37.

25. See Shanks, *Hegel vs. "Inter-Faith Dialogue"*, 49.

26. See Hegel, *Lectures on the Philosophy of Religion*, 137.

27. See Ford, *CW*, 273–303.

a society that nurtures religious differences; rather, Hegel projects that the problem with the modern world will become *indifference* toward religious faith altogether. This is a problem because faith means openness; therefore, when indifference to religion becomes a norm then we also lose the norm of being open toward and judged by God—which also requires us to be open toward our neighbors. In Shanks's words, "Faith . . . is *essentially* a relationship with God made manifest in and through a certain quality of sympathetic moral open-mindedness toward one's neighbors."[28] SR not only makes it possible to enjoy religious differences together at the same table and in the same room, but it also breaks our habit and repairs the indifference to religion—which has become a norm within modern society.

The Problem of Inter-faith Dialogue

How can Hegel's understanding of faith in his philosophy of religion help us gain traction on the question of whether SR should be called an inter-faith dialogue? Shanks provides an answer to the question of what Hegel might think of the phrase "inter-faith dialogue," and I apply some of the premises from Shanks's argument to the question of whether SR should be considered an inter-faith dialogue.

Shanks argues that Hegel would reject the phrase "inter-faith dialogue" as one that offers a proper philosophical description of what people of different religious traditions are doing if they converse or engage with one another. The first sentence of Shanks's *Hegel vs. "Inter-Faith Dialogue"* is quite direct and provocative: we should "object to the term 'inter-faith dialogue' because of what it does to the theological concept of 'faith.'"[29] The first premise against

28. Shanks, *Hegel vs. "Inter-Faith Dialogue"*, 3.

29. Shanks, *Hegel vs. "Inter-Faith Dialogue"*, 1.

the phrase "inter-faith dialogue," therefore, concerns how it becomes too reductionist concerning "the theological concept of faith."[30]

The second premise involves a distinction between a *theological understanding* of faith vs. an *ideological use* of faith. Shanks offers the distinction on these terms: "'inter-faith' is an intrinsically *xenophilia*-restrictive term, forever tending to divert true *theo*-logical consideration of religious diversity away from *xenophilia* into a merely *ideological* negotiation process, between those representing rival claims to metaphysical truth-as-correctness."[31] The Hegelian lesson here concerns how the phrase "inter-faith dialogue" assumes an *ideological use of faith*. According to Shanks, "Talk of 'inter-faith dialogue' suggests a notion of 'faiths' in the plural," and this suggestion turns faith into the kind "defined by tick-box, checklist criteria."[32] An ideological use of faith turns faith into exactly what Hegel seeks to avoid in how he constructs the concept of faith in his philosophy of religion, and the problematic use of faith is how the word "faith" usually is used in the phrase "inter-faith dialogue."[33]

Shanks's third premise turns its attention toward what a theological understanding of faith looks like. He claims, "True faith . . . only ever serves to open minds" because

30. See Shanks, *Hegel vs. "Inter-Faith Dialogue"*, 1.

31. Shanks, *Hegel vs. "Inter-Faith Dialogue"*, 1–2.

32. Shanks, *Hegel vs. "Inter-Faith Dialogue"*, 3.

33. Shanks claims that none of this is meant to deny "that much of what passes under the name of 'inter-faith dialogue' is quite admirable"; his "objection is only to that name, that way of 'placing' the enterprise; and to the way it tends to insulate the xenophile impulse at work here, diverting it towards a [reductive] mode of self-expression, which unfortunately disempowers it." Shanks, *Hegel vs. "Inter-Faith Dialogue"*, 10.

"salvation is, itself . . . , an [absolute] opening of the mind."[34] A theological understanding of faith necessarily includes salvation, and salvation involves "an opening of the mind."[35] This openness moves us beyond the contours and restrictions of inter-faith dialogue in the sense that true "faith bursts the conceptual bounds of 'inter-faith dialogue' . . . by virtue of its sheer intrinsic generosity."[36] An ideological use of faith means that faith lacks generosity and openness whereas a theological understanding of faith requires both generosity and openness.

The fourth premise becomes quite relevant to the practice of Scriptural Reasoning. According to Shanks, "[T]rue faith . . . is *in essence* an energizing of perfect truth-as-openness. Hence, it is that potential quality *specifically of Abrahamic religion in general*, which promotes . . . radical *xenophilia*."[37] Shanks admits that Hegel grasps neither Judaism nor Islam due to his cultural limitations, but Shanks thinks that Hegel sees in Judaism and Islam an understanding of faith connected with generosity and openness—specifically truth-as-openness. Whether Hegel actually sees this in Judaism and Islam matters less for my purposes than what it means for talking about the implications for Christians, Jews, and Muslims to read and study their sacred texts together. If we follow Shanks's interpretation of Hegel's philosophy of religion, then the phrase "inter-faith dialogue" does not do justice to what takes places within a SR session because members of all three traditions come together during SR in a spirit—or we might say Spirit, in the Hegelian sense—of generosity and truth-as-openness.

34. Shanks, *Hegel vs. "Inter-Faith Dialogue"*, 2.

35. Shanks, *Hegel vs. "Inter-Faith Dialogue"*, 2.

36. Shanks, *Hegel vs. "Inter-Faith Dialogue"*, 3.

37. Shanks, *Hegel vs. "Inter-Faith Dialogue"*, 5; some italics in the original and some italics added.

What does Shanks mean by *xenophilia*? By *xeno-philia*, he means "a fundamental predisposition to love the strangeness of those who are strange."[38] What does he mean by strange? He offers several categories, but the category that applies to SR concerns "those who are shaped by different intellectual, cultural, or religious traditions from one's own."[39] Following the argument of the previous chapter concerning friendship and *philia*, it seems that SR can be a practice that nurtures and promotes *xenophilia*. SR brings together and celebrates, in non-competitive ways, multiple ethnic groups, nationalities, and "those who are shaped by different intellectual, cultural, or religious traditions."[40] The intellectual differences found in SR concern different disciplines, methods, and ways of reasoning. The religious differences involve Christian, Jewish, and Muslim identities. Additionally, SR has included Confucians, Hindus, and Mormons.

Inclusion, however, is not enough on the standards of Hegelian *xenophilia*. Shanks claims that it requires "a fundamental disposition to love the strangeness" of others.[41] Would SR practitioners and theorists claim to love the strangeness in one another or of one another? Basit Koshul strongly affirms this question on his own terms:

> I had come to know a group of "strangers" and many new "strange" ideas. David Ford was among this group of "strangers," along with Peter Ochs and Daniel Hardy (of blessed memory). . . . And while I was familiar with interfaith dialogue at that time, the idea of Scriptural Reasoning was also "strange." Furthermore, while I was

38. Shanks, *Hegel vs. "Inter-Faith Dialogue"*, 5.

39. Shanks, *Hegel vs. "Inter-Faith Dialogue"*, 5.

40. Shanks, *Hegel vs. "Inter-Faith Dialogue"*, 5.

41. See Shanks, *Hegel vs. "Inter-Faith Dialogue"*, 5.

> familiar with Christianity and Judaism to some
> degree, these traditions were also "strange" in a
> very real sense because my relationship with a
> living Christian or Jew did not go beyond insti-
> tutional formality or collegiality.[42]

According to Koshul, SR nurtures a love of strangeness in one another and of one another.

Staying closer to the original Greek of the New Testament (see Romans 12 and Hebrews 13), Daniel Smith argues that SR actually achieves *philoxenia* in the sense commanded or encouraged by early Christian authors. Smith breaks down Hebrews 13:2 in this way: "Let mutual care [Greek *philadelphia*] continue; and do not neglect the care of strangers [Greek *philoxenia*], for by doing so, some extended hospitality to angels without knowing."[43] In his essay about SR, Smith's question concerns intellectual differences—can philosophers and theologians practice *philoxenia* toward scholars in biblical studies?—a question in which he affirms. Again, following the argument of the previous chapter—and Martha Nussbaum's insights about *philia*—I conclude that SR is a practice that encourages *philoxenia* or *xenophilia*.[44]

This emphasis on strangeness means that we need to be careful and cautious in how we name practices that encourage love of the strangeness of others. The risk of the strangeness needs to be captured by the phrase that we

42. Koshul, "Theology as a Vocation," 211–12.

43. See Smith, "Between Philadelphia and *Philoxenia*."

44. See Shanks, *Hegel vs. "Inter-Faith Dialogue"*, 5; see Smith, "Between Philadelphia and *Philoxenia*." Grammatically or linguistically, I prefer Smith's use of the word *philoxenia* over Shanks's use of *xenophilia*. Arguing that SR repairs *xenophobia* by cultivating *xenophilia*, however, seems to be a better move rhetorically. I am grateful to Jackson Lashier for helping me think through the implications of which word to use in this book.

choose to use. Does the phrase "inter-faith dialogue" capture this risk? Shanks answers in the negative: "The framing of the xenophile impulse under the rubric of 'inter-faith dialogue' . . . has the effect of compartmentalizing" one's faith—which neutralizes the core identity and truths of the faithful.[45] Shanks concludes, "Thus, ['inter-faith dialogue'] makes it [one's faith] too safe" in dialogues or practices with religious others.[46] To say that SR is not an "inter-faith dialogue" is simply to emphasize that SR encourages and nurtures genuine faith, the Spirit (in the Hegelian sense) to be at work during and within the practice, and truth-as-openness amongst its participants.

From the Fearfulness of Xenophobia to the Hopefulness of Xenophilia

For purposes of SR, the most important sentence in Shanks's *Hegel vs. "Inter-Faith Dialogue"* is: "[I]n his *Lectures on the Philosophy of Religion*, he sets out to survey the whole scene of human religious diversity, opening up a new space for all manner of thoughtful interaction between [members of religious] traditions."[47] What does this "new space" look like, and can SR be or become this Hegelian "new space"?[48]

According to Shanks, the "new space" involves the following: "good conversation," the priority of "mutual trust" over fear, and seeking truth communally instead of individually.[49] I contend that SR qualifies as making good conversation possible: SR encourages mutual trust and it discourages fear; SR prioritizes communal interpretations

45. See Shanks, *Hegel vs. "Inter-Faith Dialogue"*, 11.

46. See Shanks, *Hegel vs. "Inter-Faith Dialogue"*, 11.

47. Shanks, *Hegel vs. "Inter-Faith Dialogue"*, 64.

48. Shanks, *Hegel vs. "Inter-Faith Dialogue"*, 64.

49. See Shanks, *Hegel vs. "Inter-Faith Dialogue"*, 146.

of Scripture over both individual authority and individual interpretations of Scripture; SR seeks to avoid allowing one participant "to control . . . other person[s]."[50] To practice SR well, participants must "attend to other people, without seeking . . . to subdue them to [one's] will."[51] If SR seeks the truth, then it does so communally through "genuine attentiveness to other people"—and downplays the possibility of truth being known or possessed by a singular person.[52] Lastly, SR helps members of the Abrahamic religious traditions open us toward their religious neighbors—which means, on Shanks's terms, that SR cultivates and promotes a "fear-dispelling hope."[53]

Shanks argues that the shift from the fearfulness of *xenophobia* to the hopefulness of *xenophilia* requires a willingness to participate in "universal reason."[54] SR practitioners and theorists tend to express skepticism toward the notion of universalizing reason, but Shanks's explanation of the phrase harkens back to the Hebrew Prophets—specifically to Amos. Shanks claims that by the phrase "universal reason," Hegel intends to construct an aspect of prophetic reasoning: reason involves an "explosive affirmation of *xenophilia* (amongst the rich towards the poor [in Amos]) extended and . . . universalized."[55] Shanks continues, for Hegel, "'Universal Reason' means absolute truth-as-openness, recognized as the universal essence of true holiness; an attentive, genuinely ready-to-listen openness all round, towards every kind of Other without exception."[56] Hegel's

50. Shanks, *Hegel vs. "Inter-Faith Dialogue"*, 146.

51. Shanks, *Hegel vs. "Inter-Faith Dialogue"*, 146.

52. See Shanks, *Hegel vs. "Inter-Faith Dialogue"*, 146.

53. Shanks, *Hegel vs. "Inter-Faith Dialogue"*, 146.

54. Shanks, *Hegel vs. "Inter-Faith Dialogue"*, 238.

55. Shanks, *Hegel vs. "Inter-Faith Dialogue"*, 238.

56. Shanks, *Hegel vs. "Inter-Faith Dialogue"*, 238.

notion of the universalization of reason becomes the philosophical name for holding everyone to the standards of
prophetic reasoning, and prophetic reasoning requires an
"explosive affirmation of *xenophilia*."[57] For Shanks, *xenophilia* is the singular word that best captures Hegel's philosophy of religion. If Shanks is right about *xenophilia* being
the singular word that best captures Hegel's philosophy of
religion, then I infer that SR is best described as the practice
that attempts to embody and perform Hegel's philosophy
of religion—hence the "reasoning" of Scriptural Reasoning
becomes best understood as a Hegelian "xenophile 'universal reason.'"[58] If this is correct, then Shanks gives us all the
reasons we need to conclude that SR is not an "inter-faith
dialogue" since the use of "faith" in that phrase tends to neither encourage nor lead to *xenophilia*.

Conclusion

To conclude this chapter, I raise one criticism of Shanks's
argument in *Hegel vs. "Inter-Faith Dialogue"*. My difference
from Shanks's overall compelling argument concerns how
much he treats the word "faith"—in "inter-faith dialogue"—
as necessarily static. Shanks does not seek to repair the
phrase "inter-faith dialogue" but to dismiss it. I am sensitive
to this because this priority of dismissing over repairing gets
to the heart of the difference between Peirce's pragmatism
and Richard Rorty's neo-pragmatism. Peirce seeks to repair
and clarify beliefs, concepts, ideas, phrases, and words. Rorty
simply dismisses those beliefs, concepts, ideas, phrases, and
words that seem to need repair—making them beyond repair. Shanks comes much closer to Rorty's neo-pragmatism
than to Peirce's conviction to repair the phrases that we

57. See Shanks, *Hegel vs. "Inter-Faith Dialogue"*, 238.

58. Shanks, *Hegel vs. "Inter-Faith Dialogue"*, 241.

consider broken. While I am in agreement with Shanks's concerns about the phrase "inter-faith dialogue" and think it worthwhile to apply his argument to the practice of SR—and, therefore, conclude that SR is not a form of inter-faith dialogue—I also think that SR provides clues or hints for repairing all of the problematic aspects identified by Shanks in the phrase "inter-faith dialogue."

If SR practitioners and theorists wish to continue to use the phrase "inter-faith dialogue" for describing SR, then I recommend the following repairs to the phrase:

> (a) "Faith" in "inter-faith" needs to be understood as the type of faith that enhances a person's identity.

> (b) "Faith" in "inter-faith" needs to be understood as precisely what makes participants open and sympathetic with one another; the faith that participants of SR bring to the table is the cause of their openness and sympathy with one another, not an impediment to such openness and sympathy.[59]

> (c) The "inter-" in "inter-faith" needs to exhibit *xenophilia* among and between participants where the strangeness of others has the potential to lead to transformation—either behaviorally or conceptually.

> (d) "Dialogue," in "inter-faith dialogue," needs to involve more listening than talking—what Shanks describes as "genuine attentiveness to

---

59. I use the word "cause" deliberately here, and I mean by it what Donald Davidson defends and explains as "causes"—which he distinguishes from "reasons"—in Davidson, "Actions, Reasons, and Causes," 3–20. The sentence does not read: the faith that participants of SR bring to the table is the reason of their openness and sympathy with one another.

other people";[60] the talking that occurs ought to be disciplined by the shared words of the text(s) being studied together.

(e) If SR practitioners and theorists continue to use the phrase "inter-faith dialogue" to describe the practice of SR, then we need to use the phrase with an emphasis on how SR allows *xenophilia* to replace both *xenophobia* and indifference toward religious believers and religious communities.

Even given these potential repairs, I remain skeptical about calling SR an inter-faith dialogue and will continue to refer to it as an inter-religious dialogue.

---

60. Shanks, *Hegel vs. "Inter-Faith Dialogue"*, 146.

8 _____

Is Scriptural Reasoning an Inter-hope Practice?

SR *after* Caputo

> *Daring to hope, hoping against hope, having hope*
> *in the smile on the surface of matter, having the*
> *audacity to return to that smile against the dark*
> *sides of personal, social, global, solar, or cosmic*
> *death—the anatomy of that smile, the dynamics*
> *of the faith and hope that respond to that smile,*
> *the ups and downs of that smile, its promises and*
> *its threats—that is the subject matter of the reli-*
> *gion I . . . defend.*[1]

Introduction

In the previous chapter, I concluded that the practice of
SR should not be described in terms of an inter-faith dialogue. In this chapter, I construct what it means for SR to
be an inter-hope practice. SR is an inter-hope practice, but
what does that mean?

1. Caputo, *Hoping Against Hope*, 166.

The phrase inter-hope practice offers a description of SR that I have neither heard nor seen before as a description of SR.[2] The phrase itself comes from the thought of America's own Continental philosopher, John Caputo. Caputo taught philosophy for several years at Villanova University, and now he teaches in the religious studies department at Syracuse University—a move similar, I should point out, to Peter Ochs's professorial shift from philosophy to UVa's religious studies program. Caputo is known for his arguments about "radical hermeneutics," a book explicitly titled "against ethics," and his struggle over how to think with Martin Heidegger despite Heidegger's own philosophical (his Romanticist recovery of pre-Socratic philosophy) and political (his Nazism) failings. In this chapter, however, I will spend most of my time engaging with his recently published memoir, entitled *Hoping Against Hope: Confessions of a Postmodern Pilgrim.*[3]

In this chapter, I argue that the phrase inter-hope practice properly captures SR's attempt to bring together Jews, Christians, and Muslims for the purpose of a strict—perhaps even radical—hermeneutical practice. I consider ways in which SR falls in line with Caputo's expectations for an inter-hope practice—his actual phrase is "inter-hope dialogue"—and ways in which SR departs from his expectations. The gist of this difference echoes a distinction teased

2. The closest one comes is found in Nicholas Adams's "Making Deep Reasonings Public," when he describes SR as a technique of hope: "To be open to luck in the study of Scripture is to give up control in favour of patience and hope, and to view outcomes not as the result of random factors but as the endless flow of surprises made possible by . . . whatever makes surprises possible." Adams, MDRP, 48. In this passage, Adams comes very close to the description of SR as inter-hope exercise.

3. My gratitude goes to William Elkins for recommending that I bring Caputo's work in relation to SR, and we "see what happens"!

out throughout this companion: the *playfulness* of SR resembles Caputo's postmodernism, whereas the *pragmatism* of SR promises too much on Caputo's standards.

Conditional and Unconditional Hospitality

In his memoir, *Hoping Against Hope*, John Caputo offers in-depth reflections on his own religious identity throughout his life. Part of his reflections lead to a constructive account of the concept of hospitality within religious congregations and in inter-religious gatherings. His constructive account on hospitality involves a distinction between conditional and unconditional hospitality. Caputo writes:

> In conditional hospitality, we practice hospitality "by invitation only," which is a harsh, most inhospitable and exclusionary phrase. Here we have the initiative and we extend an invitation whose terms we get to decide in advance. We welcome those we have chosen in advance, so that the offer is inevitably conditioned by a lot of ulterior motives. But in unconditional hospitality, we have lost the initiative. This is not an invitation we initiate but a visitation we did not see coming, which means that something visits itself upon us, requiring an unprepared, unconditional welcome, in a kind of naked exposure to the coming of the other.[4]

In his application of this distinction to the practice of inter-religious gatherings, he argues that the "conditional way keeps our own presuppositions safe; the unconditional way puts them at risk."[5] What does this mean? Caputo clarifies

4. Caputo, *Hoping Against Hope*, 85.
5. Caputo, *Hoping Against Hope*, 91.

and elaborates on how the "conditional way keeps our own presuppositions safe":

> The safe way says, I am not entering this dialogue except under certain conditions, that is, from the standpoint of my faith, which is strong. I would not expect you to respect me if I did not, and I expect you to do the same. I am prepared to put my presuppositions at risk, but only up to a certain point, where I draw the line. I will see . . . how far I can go before the ice starts to look a little thin and I am forced to turn back. So let's see where there is overlapping agreement between us; then, after seeing where we agree, let's shake hands and agree to disagree. Let's have a drink together after the meeting is over [but] before we hit we road to return to our respective corners in the faith community from which we came, and agree not to launch another religious war.[6]

He also clarifies and elaborates on how "the unconditional way puts [our own presuppositions] at risk":

> An unconditional inter-faith dialogue, one that has some teeth, starts with what Heidegger called our "thrownness" into the world. . . . We find ourselves thrown into the place where we wake up in the world. . . . The meaning of "faith" in the conditional form of "inter-faith" takes place entirely on the level of beliefs . . . , [but belief ought] to be distinguished from faith as the condition from the unconditional. . . . Faith has to do with a deeper fidelity, a deeper responsibility to what is calling upon or visiting itself upon us unconditionally, wherever we live and whatever we believe.[7]

6. Caputo, *Hoping Against Hope*, 91.
7. Caputo, *Hoping Against Hope*, 96.

These passages raise several questions. First, what is this notion of "thrownness," and how does it apply to encounters with the "religious other"? Second, what does an inter-faith dialogue look like on Caputo's terms? Third, does SR more easily fit Caputo's description of a conditional or unconditional way of engaging with the "religious other"?

Caputo defines Heidegger's notion of thrownness in this way: "We find ourselves thrown into the place where we wake up in the world."[8] Caputo uses this Heideggerian notion to talk about the contingency of religious identity. At one point in his memoir, Caputo tells this story:

> When I was lecturing once in the Middle East, I
> met a Muslim theologian who was born and has
> spent his entire life in the Middle East, who had
> no hesitation in pointing out to me after my talk
> that were we switched at birth, I would be the
> Muslim and he would be the American Catholic
> from southwest Philadelphia. Religion cannot
> be detached from its cultural context. Religion
> is very much a matter of where we were born
> and when.[9]

In addition to the claim that religion "cannot be detached from its cultural context," we can use the Heideggeran notion of thrownness to say that religious believers cannot be detached from where they have been "thrown." According to Caputo, thrownness is "what the faithful like to call 'amazing grace.'"[10]

In reflecting on his own story, Caputo writes that perhaps "a more neutral observer would call it a not a very amazing, highly probable, and statistically predictable

8. Caputo, *Hoping Against Hope*, 96.

9. Caputo, *Hoping Against Hope*, 92–93.

10. Caputo, *Hoping Against Hope*, 93.

feature of an accident of birth."[11] Perhaps we should save "the idea of grace for something more amazing than that."[12] What could be more "amazing"? Caputo answers that it "would be much more amazing if this fellow grew up a Catholic and I a Muslim. Switched at birth, everything that is in my head and baked in my bones would be inside his, and vice-versa."[13]

While I am not convinced that the point of Heideggerian thrownness is to spend one's day considering counterfactuals, Caputo's point—I take it—concerns challenging the ways in which we tend to take a deterministic view about our own religious identities: so one is a Christian because he or she has been thrown into Christianity in terms of their particular circumstances and social contingencies; one is Jewish because he or she has been thrown into Judaism in terms of their birth parents or who they marry; one is a Muslim because he or she has been thrown into Islam in terms of their particular circumstances and social contingencies. We could play this game all day! We are "thrown" into our religious traditions, and when people from different religious traditions come together there ought to be an awareness that our religious identities are contingent on factors beyond the content of our religious beliefs.

Second, what does an inter-faith dialogue look like on Caputo's terms? Faith is not equivalent to belief. By faith, Caputo wants us to mean "a deeper fidelity, a deeper responsibility to what is calling upon or visiting itself upon us unconditionally, wherever we live and whatever we believe."[14] For an unconditional inter-faith dialogue, the faith that participants bring to the table requires them to do the following:

11. Caputo, *Hoping Against Hope*, 93.
12. Caputo, *Hoping Against Hope*, 93.
13. Caputo, *Hoping Against Hope*, 93.
14. Caputo, *Hoping Against Hope*, 97.

(a) to put their presuppositions at risk with no limits to that risk, (b) to seek neither agreement nor disagreement with other participants, and (c) to trust the practice or process of dialogue without needing the practice or process to have any results relating to one's beliefs.

Third, does SR more easily fit Caputo's description of conditional or unconditional ways of engaging with the "religious other"? Does SR have the characteristics required for Caputo's unconditional inter-faith dialogue? Or does SR have the characteristics of conditional inter-faith dialogue: (a) "to put my presuppositions at risk, but only up to a certain point, where I draw the line," (b) to look for "over-lapping agreement between us," and (c) to desire concrete results in terms of our beliefs once we complete the practice or process of dialogue?

William Stacy Johnson and Peter Ochs provide one answer to this set of questions. In their "Introduction" to the book, *Crisis, Call, and Leadership in the Abrahamic Traditions*, they argue:

> In scriptural reasoning . . . , the accent is on *interpretive hospitality*. Participants from all three traditions read, struggle over, challenge, and interpret texts from their own and the others' traditions with a sense of openness and mutuality. There may arise argument . . . —debate, discussion, questioning—but this takes place in a spirit of mutual respect and of wonder—and, throughout, of love of God's Word as embodied in our respective scriptures.[15]

From Caputo's perspective, this answer blends aspects of unconditional hospitality—argument, mutuality, openness—with conditional hospitality: the belief concerning a love for "God's Word."

15. Johnson and Ochs, "Introduction," 3.

From Faith to Hope

Caputo makes a Pauline move in his memoir when he shifts from faith to hope for talking about his expectations for inter-faith dialogue.[16] He writes:

> This deeper faith goes hand-in-hand with a more deeply lodged hope in the promise, in what is to-come, which lacks assurances about the object of our hope. Instead of inter-faith meetings—which run the risk of being trade fairs in which we browse the aisles of beliefs of others—I prefer "inter-hope" dialogues, in which we share our dreams and hopes in an effort to encourage one another. . . . Faith arises from [an] obscure and distant call, an ambiguous solicitation, and a hope in an uncertain future. It demands that we assume responsibility for a past we had nothing to do with shaping and a hope for a future we cannot control, while admitting that we have not been hard-wired in advance to The Truth.[17]

The unconditional inter-faith dialogue becomes an inter-hope dialogue, and the conditional inter-faith dialogue fails to become an inter-hope dialogue. Therefore, on Caputo's terms, SR can be considered an inter-hope dialogue if and only if it meets the earlier requirements for an unconditional inter-faith dialogue.

In addition to the characteristics for an inter-faith dialogue—(a) putting one's presuppositions at risk with no limits to that risk, (b) seeking neither agreement nor disagreement, and (c) trusting the practice or process of dialogue without needing the practice or process to have

16. I call it Pauline because, throughout his epistles, the Apostle Paul seems to think in terms of a logical progression from faith to hope and eventually to charity/love.

17. Caputo, *Hoping Against Hope*, 96–98.

any definite results—an inter-hope dialogue contains these traits: (d) taking responsibility for the past sins of the religious tradition of which we have been "thrown," (e) preparing for the future with the knowledge that it remains out of our control ("anticipation," not "expectation," is Heidegger's word for what Caputo wants), and (f) suspending claims concerning "The Truth." We should add (g) as well and use Caputo's words: "Hope is the risky business of calling for the coming of what we cannot see coming, of saying yes to the future, where nothing is guaranteed."[18]

Within SR, the claim that we ought to suspend "the Truth" during our time studying together usually comes with the Peircean understanding that we suspend The Truth because no one person possesses The Truth anyway.

In *Radical Hermeneutics*,[19] however, Caputo comes across as more aggressive about this than a Peircean would. Caputo argues that one of the obligations of dialogue involves calling people out on assumptions, claims, and interpretations that suggest knowledge of Goodness and Truth. This involves what Heidegger calls the destruction of metaphysics, and Caputo turns this destruction of metaphysics into a mode of communication where we destruct the metaphysical claims of one another. In this way, Caputo's expectations for inter-hope dialogue follows from his previously established radical hermeneutics.

18. Caputo, *Hoping Against Hope*, 199.

19. I refer to claims made in ch. 3 of Caputo's *Radical Hermeneutics*: "No interpretation is safe" (Caputo, *Radical Hermeneutics*, 73); "Where does . . . Interpretation get its clue? Heidegger responds: we *are* the beings to be investigated" (78); "Hermeneutics is on the way beyond Being, is already engaged in a destruction of ontology, an overcoming of . . . metaphysics" (85). I take all of this to mean that if interpreting texts in a public or social setting that others around you have an obligation to "destruct" the ways in which assumptions of Being, Goodness, and Truth slip into your interpretation of that text.

What would SR look like if it practiced this aspect of radical hermeneutics: calling each other out if and when passages of traditionally sacred texts get interpreted on terms of Absolute Truth, Dyadic Reasoning, or Universal Goodness?

Hope, Radical Hermeneutics, and Scriptural Reasoning

I argue that SR can meet Caputo's requirements for inter-hope dialogue, which I prefer to call an inter-hope practice (for reasons I explain later), but this does not mean that SR must submit to each of Caputo's recommended characteristics in a wholesale way.

By giving sacred texts authority over the presuppositions of all of the participants, SR achieves (a) putting one's presuppositions at risk with no limits to that risk. Nicholas Adams persuasively argues that SR meets (b): seeking neither agreement nor disagreement.[20] In relation to (c)—trusting the practice without needing to have any definite results in the end—this has been part of the tension within SR that I have raised in this book: the playful side of SR certainly achieves (c) whereas the pragmatist side of SR tends to set "definite results" and for understandable reasons. Describing SR only as playful makes it difficult—if not impossible—to find funding, gain governmental and institutional support, and recruit new practitioners. We live in a result-driven world, and SR lives in this world. SR lives in this world not only because of the world, but also because of Ochs's commitment to peace-building and pragmatism. The playful side has always been treated (by practitioners and theorists of SR) as SR's dirty little secret, but most of what scriptural reasoners enjoy about doing SR involves

20. See Adams, *Habermas and Theology*, ch. 11.

more the playfulness of the exercise than what results from the practice. SR certainly promises definite results, but these results usually are not really definite. The point of SR is the practice of reading sacred texts together and seeing what happens conversationally, hermeneutically, logically, socially, and theologically.

Do SR participants take responsibility for the past sins of their own religious traditions? Yes and no. There is some expectation for participants in SR to own bad and oppressive *interpretations* of passages from their sacred texts. For instance, for Christians to own up to anti-Semitic interpretations of Old and New Testament passages. However, SR does not seem to require treating participants as representatives of all of the bad and oppressive parts of each Abrahamic tradition. Speaking for myself, I would be baffled by a Jewish participant taking responsibility for extreme Zionism or a Muslim participant even bringing up Al-Queda or ISIS. These are the expectations of social media—for all Jews and Muslims to comment on the violent extremism of their own traditions—and, in my judgment, SR should not follow this new cultural expectation. However, SR should invite participants to admit to oppressive interpretations of certain passages in their sacred texts. This lifts up the importance of hermeneutics in relation to taking responsibility for the past sins of the religious tradition of which the participants have been "thrown."

Can SR help us prepare for the future without the need to control the future? Yes, and this proposition sums up Peter Ochs's own hope for the practice of SR. Ochs writes:

> The active voice of scriptural reasoning emerges under the banner of hope. The dialectic of modernity has died; while we are not necessarily pleased with its passing, we have hope that a new life will arise. Hope includes the vision and

expectation of renewed life. With this vision SR moves past its constative voice and practice of sad acknowledgment as it turns to envision possibility and to share the energy and excitement that new possibility brings. Hope is a word to express that excitement.[21]

SR prepares us for the peace given to us and promised by the God of Abraham, but here (2002) Ochs claims that SR in no way brings about this promise of peace. We study together, according to Ochs, because this is what the God of Abraham intends for his children to do together—which falls closer to what I have been calling the playful side of SR. This does not require a claim of Absolute Truth because it can be understood in terms of triadic reasoning: not an absolute truth claim but a theological claim that God promises peace *for* God's children.

Ochs's theological understanding of SR leads us back to Caputo's memoir. What does Caputo mean by "hope" in the phrase "inter-hope dialogue"? Caputo's answer:

Hope means that things are neither steered mightily unto good by an invisible wisdom nor hollowed out at their center by some primordial catastrophe and doomed to fail. Hope means that things are just unstable, risky, nascent, natal, betokening neither an absolute plenum nor an absolute void. . . . Hope means that the world contains an uncontainable promise, which is also a threat. Hope means that a great "perhaps" hovers over the world, that what holds sway over the world is not the Almighty but a might-be. But "perhaps" does not signify an attitude of lassitude or indifference. "Perhaps" continues a discussion that the authorities considered

21. Ochs, "Rules of Scriptural Reasoning."

> closed. "Perhaps" is not indecisive but is fueled
> by the audacity to hope.[22]

SR is a practice of "perhaps" in Caputo's sense of the word.[23] SR is a practice that comes with a set of "promises" but also potential "threats."[24] SR is a practice that not only avoids indifference but repairs the indifference about religious traditions that Hegel identifies as a problem within modernity. SR is a practice "fueled by the audacity to hope."[25] For these reasons, SR is an inter-hope practice.

Scriptural Reasoning as an Inter-hope Dialogue

The following table presents (a) characteristics for an inter-hope dialogue, (b) Caputo's clarification of the characteristics, (c) a potential response from an SR practitioner and theorist in relation to Caputo's clarification, and (d) my own conclusions concerning what the characteristic says about the playfulness of SR.

22. Caputo, *Hoping Against Hope*, 198.

23. By saying this, however, I do not want to commit SR to sharing in Caputo's full "theology of perhaps"—which he develops elsewhere. See Caputo, *Insistence of God*.

24. See Caputo, *Hoping Against Hope*, 198.

25. Caputo, *Hoping Against Hope*, 198.

Characteristics of an Inter-Hope Dialogue	Caputo	SR's Response	My Conclusion
Questioning the Metaphysical Presuppositions of Participants:	Participants should put one's metaphysical presuppositions at risk with no limits to that risk.	Adams argues that participants should be allowed their "deep reasonings" even if they are "metaphysical," but the post-metaphysical methodology of SR encourages the "logic of Scripture" to call out problematic and unnecessary metaphysical interpretations of particular passages.[26]	SR needs to allow for participants to discover their "deep reasonings" even if such reasonings are metaphysical, but participants in SR ought to prioritize playing with a variety of interpretations of a passage over their own metaphysical interpretation(s).

26. Although not in relation to the practice of SR, Morgan Elbot persuasively argues that one can hold together both Caputo's postmodernism and Habermas's post-metaphysical thinking: "Rather than seeing Habermas's postmetaphysical thinking and Caputo's postmodernism as adversaries, we should instead recognize their common enemy. Both identify a similar combatant as the hostile and destructive force to a successful relationship between philosophy and religion: Caputo's opposition to cynical disbelief is akin to Habermas's opposition to coercive will formation. Both undermine the capacity to see otherwise, to nourish an unbridled wonder about the boundless ways of being, thinking and hoping. If discourse between philosophy and religion is understood as part of the same resistance that refuses to accept the insidious modes of thought that obstruct the realization of a more self-reflexive philosophy and religion, then it just might be possible to understand the disagreement

Characteristics of an Inter-Hope Dialogue	Caputo	SR's Response	My Conclusion
Making Truth-claims During the Dialogue:	Participants are required to suspend all claims concerning "The Truth."	On the standards of Coleridgean Romanticism and Peircean pragmatism, SR should not suspend claims concerning "The Truth," but should recognize that truth cannot be possessed by individuals but found in triadic relationships.[27]	I remain skeptical that the practice of SR—which limits itself in terms of inclusion, space, and time—affords the proper conditions for making claims about "The Truth"; my reasons are not the same as Caputo's reasons, because I am thinking more along the lines of how making truth-claims during the process of SR might block further playful engagement with the words of the scriptural passages being studied.

between Caputo's postmodern radical hermeneutics and Habermas's postmetaphysical communicative rationality as nothing more than quibbles about the best way to get to the same destination." Elbot, "John Caputo and Jürgen Habermas," 10.

27. One of the clearest descriptions of the word triadic in relation to Ochs's use of it can be found in C. C. Pecknold's book on Augustine, George Lindbeck, and Peter Ochs; Pecknold explains: "One of Ochs's aims . . . is to display a triadic logic of relations within interpretive communities. . . . The triadic logic that Ochs displays . . . gives explicitly corrective and constructive philosophical guidance to a program of 'scriptural reasoning' between [Muslim], Jewish, and

Characteristics of an Inter-Hope Dialogue	Caputo	SR's Response	My Conclusion
Agreement and Disagreement between Participants:	Participants should seek neither agreement nor disagreement with one another.	Participants should seek neither agreement nor disagreement with one another.[28]	Yes, seeking neither agreement nor disagreement remains a key characteristic of the practice of SR.

Christian readers . . . and displays an openness to other religious and secular reading communities as well. Ochs turns to Peirce because he is the philosopher who offers a way of making these relations visible through a system of logical graphs that can diagram the incomplete signs or 'icons' of individuals by showing their mutual needs in relation. Peircean logic helps to correct and supplement the dyadic . . . logic of Cartesian-Kantian thought through a triadic logic of relations that displays the interdependency of signs understood in semiotic and social terms. . . . What this relational, triadic logic displays is the need for a 'third grade of clearness' which does not behind modern, that is, Cartesian 'clarity' or 'distinctness' but supplements it . . . " Pecknold, *Transforming Postliberal Theology*, 62.

28. See Adams, *Habermas and Theology*, ch. 11.

Characteristics of an Inter-Hope Dialogue	Caputo	SR's Response	My Conclusion
The Purpose-fulness of the Practice/ Process:	Participants ought to trust the dialogical process without needing that process to have any clear or definite results.	Ochs maintains a tension between playfulness and purposeful-ness; Hardy prioritizes purposefulness over playfulness; Adams thinks friendship is a definite end or result of SR.[29]	The tension keeps SR interesting to those who want a playful practice and those who want the practice to have definite ends; my own tendency is some-where in between Caputo's playful postmodernism and Ford's descrip-tion of SR as a "leisure activity."
The Past Sins of One's Religious Tradition:	Participants are required to take responsibility for the past sins of the religious tradition of which they have been "thrown."	SR does not require this, but participants can confess the past sins—in terms of identifying oppressive, problematic, and traumatic interpretations of particular passages—of their own religious traditions.[30]	Because of the intensified amount of vulnerability this requires, Caputo's version could become its own kind of SR session for a group of SR practitioners who have constantly achieved "mutual trust" together; I do not recom-mend making it a requirement for SR in general.

29. See Table 1.

30. I take this to be the point of Julia Snyder and Daniel Weiss's collection, *Scripture and Violence*; see Snyder, "Introduction: Is There

Characteristics of an Inter-Hope Dialogue	Caputo	SR's Response	My Conclusion
Relationship with the Future:	Participants prepare for the future without controlling the future.	Ochs offers a theological version of Caputo's take: we prepare for the future, and the future will be determined only by and through the promises of God.[31]	I agree with Caputo and Ochs, and I find that this offers a surprising overlap between Ochs's Jewish philosophy and Caputo's Heideggerean take on the future (anticipation over expectation).

Given my conclusions, SR ought to be considered a playful inter-hope practice.[32]

---

a Bomb in This Text?"

31. See Ochs, "Rules of Scriptural Reasoning."

32 I am grateful to Lori Branch, Jack Caputo, Morgan Elbot, Brad Stone, Matthew Vaughan, and Willie Young for their comments on an earlier draft of this chapter.

Conclusion

A Moral Perspective on
the Practice of SR

As a conclusion, I want briefly to offer a Kantian explanation of what occurs within SR sessions.[1] This allows me to conclude by reflecting on SR from a substantive moral perspective.[2] If this conclusion has a thesis statement, then it would be this: after much consideration and a change of mind on the matter,[3] deontology—not virtue theory—provides the best moral perspective for articulating what drives SR morally.[4]

1. On the relationship between SR and Kant's overall philosophical program, see Rashkover, "Scriptural Reasoning: From Text Study to Enquiry." This conclusion is partly inspired by conversations with Rashkover over the years.

2. For a different yet complementary reflection on SR from a substantive moral perspective, see Slater, "Between Comparison and Normativity," 45–66.

3. See Goodson, *Narrative Theology and the Hermeneutical Virtues*, ch. 5.

4. In "Kant and the Nature of Doctrine," I found myself heading

For the sake of both clarity and simplicity, and to follow up on assertions made in chapter 5, I describe SR through Kant's categorical imperatives: the dignity test and the universalization test (found in Kant's *Grounding for the Metaphysics of Morals*). I believe that observers and participants of SR will find these tests present at the table of study. First, the dignity test is found within the practice of SR when participants refuse to use other interlocutors as a means to their own intellectual end. I have in mind here the refusal (a) to proselytize, (b) to tell other participants what their religion really thinks, and (c) to use SR sessions strictly as a means to their own scholarly ends— i.e., participating in a session reading Genesis 1-3, Surah 7, and John 1 *only because* you are writing on creation. If participants hear or see these rules being broken, then they should call out the participant breaking them because—by doing so—the dignity of individual participants gets protected. Participants in SR should think of this set of rules less as a critique of or judgment against those who violate them (though it is that) and more as a protection of those participants whose dignity might be violated.

Second, the universalization test is found within the practice of SR—not through a process of consensus—but when participants treat the passages in front of them as sacred even when those passages come from texts that they might not consider sacred. Kant advises: act only on that maxim whereby you can at the same time will that it should become a universal law. Without the subject-centered aspects of this categorical imperative, participants in SR act toward texts in a way that allows those texts to be sacred because of the relationships those texts have with the believers in their religious traditions. I place it under

in this direction (see Goodson, "Kant and the Nature of Doctrine," footnote 19).

the heading of universalization because participants orient themselves around the assumptions of other participants—which looks like a process of submitting to the universalization of the sacredness of these texts: a Christian treats a passage from the Qur'an as sacred in the best ways that they can; a Jew treats a passage from the New Testament as sacred in the best ways that they can; etc.

Within the context of SR: *the dignity test relates to how participants treat one another during the process of arguing about and interpreting the passages in front of them whereas the universalization test relates to how the participants treat the objects of study—scriptural passages from the Tanakh, New Testament, and Qur'an—in front of them by taking those objects of study as sacred because other citizens in the world and other participants at the table of study understand those passages to be sacred.*

This use of the universalization test might not work on Kant's standards for the purpose of the categorical imperative, but I submit that the problem with Kant's standards comes about because of the subject-centered rationality that remains part and parcel of Kant's own understanding of the categorical imperatives. The version of the universalization test found within the practice of SR makes sense only when multiple relationships are taken into account: the relationships of the participants gathered around these sacred texts as objects of study and the responsibility that the participants have to take seriously the beliefs of the religious traditions that nurture these texts as sacred. These religious traditions have to consent neither to the practice of SR nor the content of the arguments that arise during a SR session, but the participants in SR consent to the belief that these texts are sacred within particular communities and traditions.

In other words, and returning to Habermas's theory of communicative rationality, SR reverses the direction of consent required within Habermas's theory: SR does not expect religious traditions to consent to the interpretations made through the practice of SR—which would be an impossible expectation given that SR does not seek a final, singular interpretation—but, rather, SR expects its participants to consent to the sacredness of the texts in front of its participants. To the extent that (a) the universalization test requires Kant's defense of the unconditional goodness of the will and (b) the unconditional goodness of the will can be translated into a relational-centered rationality, the universalization test can be observed within SR when its participants act with *good will* toward the passages being studied together. By universalization, I mean thinking communicatively outside of one's own convictions in a good will effort to enter into argumentation and conversation on the terms of others—those terms being set by the sacred texts shared and studied by all during a SR session. In my judgment, SR can be understood as a playful practice that implements the rule of the dignity test—which ought to be directed toward one another— and rule of the universalization test—directed toward the texts shared and studied together. SR is a deontologically-driven, rule-based inter-religious practice that allows, encourages, and nurtures members from different religious traditions to read and study their sacred texts together and to see what happens in and within the exchanges as well as to be surprised by and to wonder at one's own sacred text and the sacred texts of others.

Bibliography

Adams, Nicholas. *Eclipse of Grace: Divine and Human Action in Hegel.*
Malden, MA: Wiley-Blackwell, 2013.

———. *Habermas and Theology.* New York: Cambridge University
Press, 2006.

———. "Making Deep Reasonings Public." In *The Promise of
Scriptural Reasoning*, edited by David F. Ford and C. C. Pecknold,
41–57. Malden, MA: Blackwell, 2006.

Anjum, Zafar. *Iqbal: The Life of a Poet, Philosopher, and Politician.*
New York: Random House, 2014.

Aquinas, Thomas. *Commentary on Aristotle's Metaphysics.* Translated
by Richard J. Blackwell. South Bend: Dumb Ox, 1995.

Arberry, Arthur J. *The Koran Interpreted.* London: Allen & Unwin,
1955.

Aristotle. *Metaphysics.* Translated by W. D. Ross. 1908. http://classics.
mit.edu/Aristotle/metaphysics.html.

———. *Nichomachean Ethics.* Translated by W. D. Ross. 1908. http://
classics.mit.edu/Aristotle/nicomachaen.html.

———. *Poetics.* Translated by S. H. Butcher. 1705. http://classics.mit.
edu/Aristotle/poetics.html.

Bailey, Jeffrey W. "New Models for Religion in Public: Inter-faith
Friendship and the Politics of Scriptural Reasoning." *The
Christian Century* 123 (2006). https://www.interfaith.cam.ac.uk/
resources/scripturalreasoningresources/newmodels.

Bibliography

Brent, Joseph. *Charles Sanders Peirce: A Life*. Bloomington: Indiana University Press, 1993.

Caputo, John D. *Hoping Against Hope: Confessions of a Postmodern Pilgrim*. Minneapolis: Fortress, 2015.

———. *The Insistence of God: A Theology of Perhaps*. Bloomington: Indiana University Press, 2013.

———. *Radical Hermeneutics: Repetition, Deconstruction, and the Hermeneutic Project*. Bloomington: Indiana University Press, 1987.

Chouliaraki, Lilie. "Mediating Vulnerability: Cosmopolitanism and the Public Sphere." *Media, Culture, & Society* 35 (2013) 105–12.

Coleridge, Samuel Taylor. *Opus Maximum*. Vol. 15 of *Collected Works of Samuel Taylor Coleridge*. Edited by Thomas McFarland. Princeton: Princeton University Press, 2002.

Corrington, Robert. *The Community of Interpreters: On the Hermeneutics of Nature and the Bible in the American Philosophical Tradition*. Macon, GA: Mercer University Press, 1996.

Dault, David. "Catholic Reasoning and Reading Across Traditions." In *Interreligious Reading after Vatican II: Scriptural Reasoning, Comparative Theology, and Receptive Ecumenism*, edited by David F. Ford and Frances Clemson, 46–61. Malden, MA: Wiley-Blackwell, 2013.

Davidson, Donald. "Actions, Reasons, and Causes." In *Essays on Actions and Events*, 3–20. 2nd ed. New York: Oxford University Press, 2001.

Diagne, Souleymane Bachir. "Achieving Humanity: Convergence between Henri Bergson and Muhammad Iqbal." In *Muhammad Iqbal: Essays on the Reconstruction of Modern Muslim Thought*, edited by H. C. Hillier and Basit Bilal Koshul, 33–55. Edinburgh: Edinburgh University Press, 2015.

———. *Islam and Open Society: Fidelity and Movement in the Philosophy of Muhammad Iqbal*. Oxford: Council for the Development of Social Science Research in Africa, 2010.

Eco, Umberto. *The Limits of Interpretation*. Bloomington: University of Indiana Press, 1991.

Edgar, Andrew. *Habermas: The Key Concepts*. New York: Routledge, 2006.

Elbot, Morgan. "John Caputo and Jürgen Habermas on Philosophy and Religion's Postmetaphysical Relationship." Unpublished paper.

Bibliography

Elkins, William, and Kurt Anders Richardson, eds. *Journal of Scriptural Reasoning: Special Issue on the Rules of Scriptural Reasoning* 2.1 (2002). https://jsr.shanti.virginia.edu/back-issues/volume-2-no-1-may-2002-the-rules-of-scriptural-reasoning/.

Farneth, Molly. "Nicholas Adams and G. W. F. Hegel on God, Community, and the Endurance of Difference." *Journal of Scriptural Reasoning* 14.2 (2015). https://jsr.shanti.virginia.edu/back-issues/vol-14-no-2-november-2015-philosophy-and-theology/nicholas-adams-and-g-w-f-hegel-god-community-and-the-endurance-of-difference/.

Ferber, Michael. *Romanticism: A Very Short Introduction*. New York: Oxford University Press, 2010.

Ford, David. *Christian Wisdom: Desiring God and Learning in Love*. New York: Cambridge University Press, 2007.

———. "Developing Scriptural Reasoning Further." In *Scripture, Reason, and the Contemporary Islam-West Encounter: Studying the "Other," Understanding the "Self"*, edited by Basit Bilal Koshul and Steven Kepnes, 201–20. New York: Palgrave Macmillan, 2007.

———. "An Interfaith Wisdom." In *The Promise of Scriptural Reasoning*, edited by David F. Ford and C. C. Pecknold, 1–22. Malden, MA: Blackwell, 2006.

———. "Paul Ricoeur: A Biblical Philosopher on Jesus." In *Jesus and Philosophy: New Essays*, edited by Paul K. Moser, 169–93. New York: Cambridge University Press, 2008.

Frei, Hans. *The Eclipse of Biblical Narrative: A Study in Eighteenth and Nineteenth Century Hermeneutics*. New Haven: Yale University Press, 1980.

Geddes, Jennifer. "Peacemaking Among the Abrahamic Faiths: An Interview with Peter Ochs." *The Hedgehog Review* 6 (2004) 90–102.

Gibbs, Robert. "Reading with Others: Levinas's Ethics and Scriptural Reasoning." In *The Promise of Scriptural Reasoning*, edited by David F. Ford and C. C. Pecknold, 171–84. Malden, MA: Blackwell, 2006.

Goodson, Jacob L., ed. *American Philosophers Read Scripture*. Lanham, MD: Lexington, 2020.

———. "Communicative Reason and Religious Faith in Secular and Post-Secular Contexts." In *The Oxford Handbook of Secularism*, edited by Phil Zuckerman and John R. Shook, 316–32. New York: Oxford University Press, 2017.

———. *The Dark Years?: Philosophy, Politics, and the Problem of Predictions*. Eugene, OR: Cascade, 2020.

———. "Hoping Against Hope." *Perspective in Religious Studies* 47 (2020) 51–68.

———. "Kant and the Nature of Doctrine: A Rule Theory Approach to Theological Reasoning." *Journal of Scriptural Reasoning* 16.1 (2017). https://jsr.shanti.virginia.edu/back-issues/volume-16-no-1-june-2017-recent-reflections-on-scriptural-reasoning/kant-and-the-nature-of-doctrine-a-rule-theory-approach-to-theological-reasoning/.

———. *Narrative Theology and the Hermeneutical Virtues: Humility, Patience, Prudence*. Lanham, MD: Lexington, 2015.

———. "'Philosophy' in *The Varieties of Religious Experience*: From Theology through the Science of Religions to a Science of Convictions." *Streams of William James* 5 (2003) 2–7. https://journal.wjsociety.org/wp-content/uploads/2014/03/Streams_5.3.pdf.

———. "Prudence in the 21st Century? Moving Beyond the Morality-Prudence Distinction with Maimonides and Rorty." In *Rorty and the Prophetic: Jewish Engagements with a Jewish Philosopher*, edited by Jacob L. Goodson and Brad Elliott Stone, chapter 2. Lanham, MD: Lexington, 2020.

———. "Repressing Novelty?: William James and the Reasoning of Scriptural Reasoning." *Journal of Scriptural Reasoning* 8.2 (2009). http://jsr.shanti.virginia.edu/back-issues/vol-8-no-2-august-2009-the-roots-of-scriptural-reasoning/repressing-novelty-william-james-and-the-reasoning-of-scriptural-reasoning/.

———. "Richard Rorty and Scriptural Reasoning." In *Rorty and the Religious: Christian Engagements with a Secular Philosopher*, edited by Jacob L. Goodson and Brad Elliott Stone, 119–39. Eugene, OR: Cascade, 2012.

———. *Strength of Mind: Courage, Hope, Freedom, Knowledge*. Eugene, OR: Cascade, 2018.

———. "'What Should I Read to Learn about Scriptural Reasoning?': An Appreciative Review of Higton and Muers's *The Text in Play*." *Journal of Scriptural Reasoning* 14.1 (2015). https://jsr.shanti.virginia.edu/back-issues/vol-14-number-1-june-2015-politics-scripture-and-war/what-should-i-read-to-learn-about-scriptural-reasoning-an-appreciative-review-of-higtons-and-muerss-the-text-in-play/.

Bibliography

Goodson, Jacob L., and Brad Elliott Stone. *Introducing Prophetic Pragmatism: A Dialogue on Hope, the Philosophy of Race, and the Spiritual Blues*. Lanham, MD: Lexington, 2019.

Greggs, Tom. "Peoples of the Covenants: Evangelical Theology and the Plurality of the Covenants in Scripture." *Journal of Scriptural Reasoning* 11.1 (2012). http://jsr.shanti.virginia.edu/back-issues/volume-11-no-1-august-2012/peoples-of-the-covenants-evangelical-theology-and-the-plurality-of-the-covenants-in-scripture/.

Greggs, Tom, et al., eds. *The Vocation of Theology Today: A Festschrift for David Ford*. Eugene, OR: Cascade, 2013.

Habermas, Jürgen. *Autonomy and Solidarity: Interviews with Jürgen Habermas*. Edited and translated by Peter Dews. Brooklyn, NY: Verso, 1992.

———. *The Divided West*. Translated by Ciaran Cronin. Malden, MA: Polity, 2006.

———. *Justification and Application: Remarks on Discourse Ethics*. Translated by Ciaran Cronin. Cambridge: MIT Press, 1993.

———. *Knowledge and Human Interests*. Translated by Jeremy J. Shapiro. Boston: Beacon, 1972.

———. *Legitimation Crisis*. Translated by Thomas McCarthy. Boston: Beacon, 1975.

———. *The Philosophical Discourse of Modernity: Twelve Lectures*. Translated by Frederick G. Lawrence. Cambridge: MIT Press, 1990.

———. *Truth and Justification*. Translated by Barbara Fultner. Malden, MA: Polity, 2003.

Hackett, Chris. "The Clasp of the Catena: The Circle and Diameter, or, How to Make Our Eschatology Clear." *Journal of Scriptural Reasoning* 8.2 (2009). http://jsr.shanti.virginia.edu/back-issues/vol-8-no-2-august-2009-the-roots-of-scriptural-reasoning/the-clasp-of-the-catena-the-circle-and-diameter-or-how-to-make-our-eschatology-clear/#_ftnref33.

Hardy, Daniel. "Harmony and Mutual Implication in the *Opus Maximum*." In *Coleridge's Assertion of Religion: Essays on the "Opus Maximum"*, edited by Jeffrey W. Barbeau, 33–52. Leuven: Peeters, 2006.

———. "The Promise of Scriptural Reasoning." In *The Promise of Scriptural Reasoning*, edited by David F. Ford and C. C. Pecknold, 185–207. Malden, MA: Blackwell, 2006.

———. "Reason, Wisdom and the Interpretation of Scripture." In *Reading Texts, Seeking Wisdom: Scripture and Theology*, edited by David F. Ford and Graham Stanton, 69–88. Grand Rapids: Eerdmans, 2004.

Hauerwas, Stanley. "A Conversation with Stanley Hauerwas on Peace and War after Scriptural Reasoning." *Journal of Scriptural Reasoning* 8.1 (2009). http://jsr.shanti.virginia.edu/back-issues/vol-8-no-1-january-2009-reason-scripture-and-war/postscript-a-conversation-with-stanley-hauerwas-on-peace-and-war-after-scriptural-reasoning/.

Hauerwas, Stanley, and Charles Pinches. "Friendship and Fragility." In *Christians among the Virtues: Theological Conversations with Ancient and Modern Ethics*, 70–88. Notre Dame: University of Notre Dame Press, 1997.

Hegel, G. W. F. *Faith and Knowledge*. Translated by Walter Cerf and H. S. Harris. Albany: State University of New York Press, 1988.

———. *Lectures on the Philosophy of Religion*. Translated by Peter Hodgson. Berkeley: University of California Press, 1998.

———. *Phenomenology of Spirit*. Translated by A. V. Miller. New York: Oxford University Press, 1977.

Heidegger, Martin. *Being and Time*. Translated by Joan Stambaugh. Albany: State University of New York Press, 2010.

Higton, Mike, and Rachel Muers. *The Text in Play: Experiments in Reading Scripture*. Eugene, OR: Cascade, 2012.

Iqbal, Muhammad. *The Reconstruction of Religious Thought in Islam*. Stanford: Stanford University Press, 2013.

James, William. *The Varieties of Religious Experience: A Study in Human Nature*. New York: Penguin, 1994.

Johnson, William Stacy, and Peter Ochs. "Introduction." In *Crisis, Call, and Leadership in the Abrahamic Traditions*, edited by Peter Ochs and William Stacy Johnson, 1–10. New York: Palgrave Macmillan, 2009.

Kant, Immanuel. *Critique of Judgment*. Translated by James Creed Meredith. New York: Oxford University Press, 2007.

———. *Critique of Pure Reason*. Translated by Max Müller and Marcus Weigelt. New York: Penguin, 2008.

———. *Grounding for the Metaphysics of Morals*. 3rd ed. Translated by James W. Ellington. Indianapolis: Hackett, 1993.

———. "What Is Enlightenment?" In *The Basic Writings of Kant*, translated by Allen Wood, 133–41. New York: Random House, 2001.

Kavka, Martin. "Is Scriptural Reasoning Senseless?" In *Scripture, Reason, and the Contemporary Islam-West Encounter: Studying the "Other," Understanding the "Self"*, edited by Basit Bilal Koshul and Steven Kepnes, 133–48. New York: Palgrave Macmillan, 2007.

Kepnes, Steven. "A Handbook for Scriptural Reasoning." In *The Promise of Scriptural Reasoning*, edited by David F. Ford and C. C. Pecknold, 23–39. Malden, MA: Blackwell, 2006.

———. "Islam as Our Other, Islam as Ourselves." In *Scripture, Reason, and the Contemporary Islam-West Encounter: Studying the "Other," Understanding the "Self"*, edited by Basit Bilal Koshul and Steven Kepnes, 107–22. New York: Palgrave Macmillan, 2007.

Kierkegaard, Søren. "You Shall Love Your *Neighbor*." In *Other Selves: Philosophers on Friendship*, edited by Michael Pakaluk, 233–47. Indianapolis: Hackett, 1991.

Koshul, Basit Bilal. "The Contemporary Relevance of Muhammad Iqbal." In *Muhammad Iqbal: Essays on the Reconstruction of Modern Muslim Thought*, edited by H. C. Hillier and Basit Bilal Koshul, 56–87. Edinburgh: Edinburgh University Press, 2015.

———. "The Qur'anic Self, the Biblical Other and the Contemporary Islam-West Encounter." In *Scripture, Reason, and the Contemporary Islam-West Encounter: Studying the "Other," Understanding the "Self"*, edited by Basit Bilal Koshul and Steven Kepnes, 9–38. New York: Palgrave Macmillan, 2007.

———. "The Rules of Scriptural Reasoning." *Journal of Scriptural Reasoning* 2.1 (2002). http://jsr.shanti.virginia.edu/back-issues/volume-2-no-1-may-2002-the-rules-of-scriptural-reasoning/editors-introduction/.

———. "Scriptural Reasoning and the Philosophy of Social Science." In *The Promise of Scriptural Reasoning*, edited by David F. Ford and C. C. Pecknold, 139–57. Malden, MA: Blackwell, 2006.

———. "Theology as a Vocation: A Weberian Perspective." In *The Vocation of Theology Today*, edited by Tom Greggs, Rachel Muers, and Simeon Zahl, 211–27. Eugene, OR: Cascade, 2013.

LaCocque, André, and Paul Ricoeur. *Thinking Biblically: Exegetical and Hermeneutical Studies*. Chicago: University of Chicago Press, 1998.

Lamberth, David. "Assessing Peter Ochs through *Peirce, Pragmatism, and the Logic of Scripture*." *Modern Theology* 24 (2008) 459–67.

Long, D. Stephen. *Speaking of God: Truth, Theology, Language*. Grand Rapids: Eerdmans, 2009.

Menand, Louis. *The Metaphysical Club: A Story of Ideas in America*. New York: Farrar, Straus & Giroux, 2002.

Bibliography

Mermer, Yamine. "Islam: A Dissenting Prophetic Voice within the Modern World." In *Scripture, Reason, and the Contemporary Islam-West Encounter: Studying the "Other," Understanding the "Self"*, edited by Basit Bilal Koshul and Steven Kepnes, 69–104. New York: Palgrave Macmillan, 2007.

Milbank, John. *Theology and Social Theory: Beyond Secular Reason.* 2nd ed. Malden, MA: Blackwell, 2006.

Miner, Robert. *Truth in the Making: Creative Knowledge in Philosophy and Theology.* New York: Routledge, 2004.

Moyaert, Marianne. *In Response to the Religious Other: Ricoeur and the Fragility of Interreligious Encounters.* Lanham, MD: Lexington, 2014.

———. "Ricoeur, Interreligious Literacy, and Scriptural Reasoning." *Studies in Interreligious Dialogue* 27 (2017) 3–26.

———. "Scriptural Reasoning as Inter-religious Dialogue." In *The Wiley-Blackwell Companion to Inter-religious Dialogue*, edited by Catherine Cornille, 64–86. New York: Blackwell, 2013.

Nussbaum, Martha. *The Fragility of Goodness: Luck and Ethics in Greek Tragedy and Philosophy.* New York: Cambridge University Press, 1986.

———. *The New Religious Intolerance: Overcoming the Politics of Fear in an Anxious Age.* Cambridge: Belknap, 2013.

Ochs, Peter. *Another Reformation: Postliberal Christianity and the Jews.* Grand Rapids: Brazos, 2011.

———. "Charles Sanders Peirce." In *Founders of Constructive Postmodern Philosophy: Peirce, James, Bergson, Whitehead, and Hartshorne*, 43–87. Albany: State University of New York Press, 1993.

———. "An Introduction to Postcritical Scriptural Interpretation." In *The Return to Scripture in Judaism and Christianity: Essays in Postcritical Scriptural Interpretation*, edited by Peter Ochs, 1–53. 1993. Reprint, Eugene, OR: Wipf & Stock, 2008.

———. "Iqbal, Peirce, and Modernity." In *Muhammad Iqbal: A Contemporary*, edited by Muhammad Suheyl Umar and Basit Bilal Koshul, 79–94. Lahore, Pakistan: Iqbal Academy, 2008.

———. "Max Kadushin as Rabbinic Pragmatist." In *Understanding the Rabbinic Mind: Essays on the Hermeneutic of Max Kadushin*, edited by Peter Ochs, 165–96. Atlanta: Scholars, 1990.

———. *Peirce, Pragmatism, and the Logic of Scripture.* New York: Cambridge University Press, 1998.

Bibliography

———. "Philosophic Warrants for Scriptural Reasoning." In *The Promise of Scriptural Reasoning*, edited by David F. Ford and C. C. Pecknold, 121–38. Malden, MA: Blackwell, 2006.

———. "Pragmatic Cataphasis: Plenitude and Caution in Morning Prayer (Taking Up Daniel Weiss' Challenge)." *Journal of Textual Reasoning* 5.1 (2007). http://jtr.shanti.virginia.edu/volume-5-number-1/pragmatic-cataphasis-plenitude-and-caution-in-morning-prayer-taking-up-daniel-weiss-challenge/.

———. *Religion without Violence: The Philosophy and Practice of Scriptural Reasoning*. Eugene, OR: Cascade, 2019.

———, ed. *The Return to Scripture in Judaism and Christianity: Essays in Postcritical Scriptural Interpretation*. 1993. Reprint, Eugene, OR: Wipf & Stock, 2008.

———. "The Rules of Scriptural Reasoning." *Journal of Scriptural Reasoning* 2.1 (2002). http://jsr.shanti.virginia.edu/back-issues/volume-2-no-1-may-2002-the-rules-of-scriptural-reasoning/the-society-of-scriptural-reasoning-the-rules-of-scriptural-reasoning7/.

Ochs, Peter, and Nancy Levene, eds. *Textual Reasonings: Jewish Philosophy and Text Study at the End of the Twentieth Century*. Grand Rapids: Eerdmans, 2003.

Ozturk, Sevcan. *Becoming a Genuine Muslim: Kierkegaard and Muhammad Iqbal*. New York: Routledge, 2018.

Pecknold, C. C. "Democracy and the Politics of the Word: Stout and Hauerwas on Democracy and Scripture." *Scottish Journal of Theology* 59 (2006) 198–209.

———. *Transforming Postliberal Theology: George Lindbeck, Pragmatism, Scripture*. New York: T. & T. Clark International, 2005.

Peirce, Charles Sanders. "How to Make Our Ideas Clear." In *The Essential Peirce, Volume 1: Selected Philosophical Writings, 1867–1893*, edited by Nathan Houser and Christian Kloesel, 124–40. Bloomington: Indiana University Press, 1992.

———. "The Nature of Meaning." In *Selected Philosophical Writings, 1893–1913*, edited by the Peirce Edition Project, 208–25. The Essential Peirce 2. Bloomington: Indiana University Press, 1998.

———. "A Neglected Argument for the Reality of God." In *The Essential Peirce, Vol. 2: Selected Philosophical Writings, 1893–1913*, edited by the Peirce Edition Project, 434–50. Bloomington: Indiana University Press, 1998.

———. "What Is Christian Faith?" In *The Collected Papers of Charles Sanders Peirce*, edited by Charles Hartshorne and Paul Weiss, 4:435–48. Cambridge: Harvard University Press, 1935.

———. "What Pragmatism Is." In *Selected Philosophical Writings, 1893–1913*, edited by the Peirce Edition Project, 331–35. The Essential Peirce 2. Bloomington: Indiana University Press, 1998.

Plato. *Euthyphro*. Translated by Benjamin Jowett. 1893. http://classics.mit.edu/Plato/euthyfro.html.

———. *The Laws*. Translated by Benjamin Jowett. 1893. http://classics.mit.edu/Plato/laws.html.

———. *Phaedrus*. Translated by Benjamin Jowett. 1893. http://classics.mit.edu/Plato/phaedrus.html.

———. *Republic*. Translated by Benjamin Jowett. 1983. http://classics.mit.edu/Plato/republic.html.

———. *Theaetetus*. Translated by Benjamin Jowett. 1893. *http://classics.mit.edu/Plato/theatu.html.*

Rashkover, Randi. "Scriptural Reasoning: From Text Study to Enquiry." *Journal of Scriptural Reasoning* 16.1 (2017). https://jsr.shanti.virginia.edu/back-issues/volume-16-no-1-june-2017-recent-reflections-on-scriptural-reasoning/scriptural-reasoning-from-text-study-to-inquiry/.

Ricoeur, Paul. *Essays in Biblical Interpretation*. Edited by Lewis S. Mudge. Philadelphia: Fortress, 1980.

———. *Figuring the Sacred: Religion, Narrative, and Imagination*. Minneapolis: Fortress, 1995.

———. *Oneself as Another*. Translated by Kathleen Blamey. Chicago: University of Chicago Press, 1992.

———. *The Symbolism of Evil*. Translated by Emerson Buchanan. Boston: Beacon, 1986.

Rockmore, Tom. "The Epistemological Promise of Pragmatism." In *Habermas and Pragmatism*, edited by Mitchell Aboulafia et al., 47–64. New York: Routledge, 2002.

Rogers, William. *Interpreting Interpretation: Textual Hermeneutics as an Ascetic Discipline*. University Park: Pennsylvania State University Press, 1994.

Schleiermacher, Friedrich. *Hermeneutics and Criticism*. Edited and translated by Andrew Bowie. New York: Cambridge University Press, 1998.

Shanks, Andrew. *Hegel vs. "Inter-Faith Dialogue": A General Theory of True Xenophilia*. New York: Cambridge University Press, 2015.

Slater, Gary. "Between Comparison and Normativity: Scriptural Reasoning and Religious Ethics." In *Scripture, Tradition, and*

Bibliography

Reason in Christian Ethics, edited by Bharat Ranganathan and Derek Alan Woodard-Lehman, 45–66. New York: Palgrave Macmillan, 2019.

———. *"Charlottesville Pragmatism."* In *Rorty and the Prophetic: Jewish Engagements with a Secular Philosopher,* edited by Jacob L. Goodson and Brad Elliott Stone, chapter 3. Lanham, MD: Lexington, 2020.

———. *C. S. Peirce and the Nested Continua Model of Religious Interpretation.* New York: Oxford University Press, 2015.

Smith, Daniel. "Between Philadelphia and Philoxenia: Finding Space in Scriptural Reasoning for 'Hospitable' Readings in Biblical Studies." *Journal of Scriptural Reasoning* 9.1 (2010). http://jsr. shanti.virginia.edu/back-issues/vol-9-no-1-december-2010-the-fruits-of-scriptural-reasoning/between-philadelphia-and-philoxenia/.

Snyder, Julia. "Introduction: Is There a Bomb in This Text?" In *Scripture and Violence,* edited by Julia Snyder and Daniel Weiss, 1–21. New York: Routledge, 2020.

Stout, Jeffrey. *Democracy and Tradition.* Princeton: Princeton University Press, 2004.

Taylor, Charles. "Preface." In *Islam and Open Society: Fidelity and Movement in the Philosophy of Muhammad Iqbal,* by Souleymane Bachir Diagne, xi–xii. Translated by Melissa McMahon. Oxford: Council for the Development of Social Science Research in Africa, 2010.

Vaughan, Matthew. "Scriptural Reasoning as (Inter)Religious Education." PhD diss., Union Theological Seminary, 2015.

White, Stephen K. "Post-structuralism and Political Reflection." *Political Theory* 16 (1988) 186–208.

Subject Index

Subject Index

Subject Index

Name Index

Name Index